YOLK

A guide to connection in
this life and beyond

Bernadette Somers

To my children
Joshua, Benjamin, Annelise and Jake.
I love you forever.
I brought you into this life,
But you brought me to life.

To Mark,
For your unwavering belief in me.
Love you dearly.

'There is a crack in everything,
that's how the light gets in'

LEONARD COHEN

Never dull the brilliance of your colours.
Shine light on all your imperfections
Always anchor to your own truth.
Embrace fear to challenge you
Lead with love front and centre.

BERNADETTE SOMERS

First published in 2019 by Bernadette Somers
bernadettesomers.com

© Bernadette Somers 2019

The moral rights of the author have been asserted

All rights reserved. Except as permitted under the *Australian Copyright Act 1968* (for example, a fair dealing for the purposes of study, research, criticism or review), no part of this book may be reproduced, stored in a retrieval system, communicated or transmitted in any form or by any means without prior written permission.

All inquiries should be made to the author.

A catalogue entry for this book is available from the National Library of Australia.

ISBN: 978-1-925921-27-4

Printed in Australia by McPherson's Printing
Project management and text design by Michael Hanrahan Publishing
Cover design by Australian artist Chloe Planinsek

The paper this book is printed on is certified as environmentally friendly.

Disclaimer: The material in this publication is of the nature of general comment only, and does not represent professional advice. It is not intended to provide specific guidance for particular circumstances and it should not be relied on as the basis for any decision to take action or not take action on any matter which it covers. Readers should obtain professional advice where appropriate, before making any such decision. To the maximum extent permitted by law, the author and publisher disclaim all responsibility and liability to any person, arising directly or indirectly from any person taking or not taking action based on the information in this publication.

Contents

Preface ix

Definitions xi

Introduction 1
    The story of Bill 7

Chapter 1: Discovering my yolk 15
    Wearing the shoes 18
    Not an easy ride 21
    Are you ready to play? 22

Chapter 2: Loving your yolk 25
    Our shells 25
    Self-love 27
    God in the yolk 30
    The story of Clare 34
    The board game of life 37
    We are exactly where we are meant to be 39
    Bypassing the white 42
    The story of Kev 45
    Yolk Practices 50

Chapter 3: Understanding your shell 53
    Appearance 54
    Gender 57
    Age 60
    The story of Ellen 62
    The shell of social media 65

Chapter 4: Expressing your yolk 67

A life without fear 67
The parent yolk 75
The story of Cathy 78
The School of Yolk 82
The story of Margot 87
Yolk Practices 90

Chapter 5: Cultivating your yolk 93

Mindfulness 95
Nature 100
The story of Jim 103
Creativity 106
Giving 110
The story of William and Connie 113
Relationships 117
The story of Louise and Rayya 119
Health 122
The story of Ella 128
Spirituality 132
Yolk Practices 135

Chapter 6: The everlasting yolk 139

The story of Mark 145
The story of Nell 149
The story of John 153
Yolk Practices 156

Conclusion 161

Preface

WRITING THIS BOOK has been a joy. It has also been a major exercise in exposing my own yolk. Every word, every sentence is a direct expression of me, laid bare for judgement and scrutiny. It is by far the most vulnerable position I have ever put myself in.

But being vulnerable means having the courage to express my yolk, share my story and wisdom, and hopefully help you access the wonder of your own yolk.

This book is not about me the messenger but rather all about the message.

Sometimes we have to venture out of our circle of fear to push ourselves to rise, to risk judgement in order to serve, to believe in ourselves, believe in our message and believe it's worth sharing. I could stay small within my shell and never take this risk, or I can write, share and give of myself so that it might resonate with you.

So, you get to pause and ponder, so you can find the quiet time to read and reflect, so that within the pages of this book you will discover the absolute majesty of your own yolk. The yolk you were born with, and take with you when you die.

This book is my message, but also a message that is beyond just me. It's wisdom beyond what I myself could offer. It's a code, a guidebook, a manual, a lighthouse.

It's through me that pen reaches paper but it's so much bigger than me. It's a universal message and I am nothing more than a humble and very grateful messenger through which this message unfolds.

Definitions

Yolk (egg): the yellow internal part of an egg.

Yolk (you): the central core of you, your essence; where all your best bits lie, the sum total of all your best qualities, attributes and talents. Your creative centre, your heart, your soul, the God or godliness that exists in you. Your true, authentic self. Your higher self.

The yolk is formless, majestic; it guides and leads you.

It is bright and crystal clear, luminous and light filled. It embodies all your essence and joy. It's flexible and timeless, a flame that never is extinguished. It sits at the very core of you, the absolute centre of your being. It draws you inward and steadies you, keeping you on course. It's coloured as you see it; bright and vibrant in any or every colour of the rainbow. It's your beacon of light and hope, your deepest desires, your every fibre and thread. It nudges you forward with love and support, it calms and nurtures you. It is your love, your light and your soul. It whispers to you words of infinite encouragement. It holds anchor for you no matter what life throws at you. It is timeless, fearless, ageless, and everlasting. It stays with you in this life and guides you home to the afterlife.

Shell (egg): the thin, hard outer layer skin of an egg.

Shell (you): your external armour, your shield, the layers that shield you from going within. Your appearance, your mask, your body, your barrier; the fear you hide behind. Your inauthenticity.

It is rigid, stuck and stagnant, controlling, unyielding, full of resistance and force. It binds you tight and limits your growth and flexibility. It is linear and bordered with restraint and constraint. It stifles your movement and freedom. It keeps you small, shackled and constricted. It is embedded with fear and hardened with control. It hinders all growth and progress. It blocks you from infinite possibility and potential. It buries your emotions. It holds you in the superficial layers that disconnect you from experiencing life to the fullest. It is clouds instead of sunlight, grey instead of white, murky and dense instead of clear.

It stands in the way of you finding you, and you may not even realise.

Introduction

WHAT IS YOUR YOLK, and how do you discover it?

This book is like a roadmap designed to help you find *you*. To help you discover your yolk, the qualities and traits you were born with that make you an authentic individual. The words in these pages are meant to get you thinking and reflecting so you can really get in touch with who you are and what really matters.

This book should be a journey of self-discovery, urging you to find who you truly are, what you are here for and what you are meant to achieve in your lifetime. It is the road to waking up and finding centre, and the road to awakening.

The chapters of the book take you through a step-by-step guide on how to discover your yolk, love it, proudly show it and cultivate it to achieve happiness and fulfilment.

It will hopefully make you discover who you are, how you tick and what floats your boat. It will help you to explore what creative talents need to be expressed, what vulnerabilities need to be exposed, and what practices need to be cultivated to get more in touch, more connected with you. It teaches you how to tap into *you*; how to show up for you; how to stretch yourself in order to grow.

With all this discovery, you hopefully will learn to unequivocally love every inch of you, to love your yolk. Self-love is the absolute essential ingredient needed to live an authentically happy life. So, I ask you to read these pages with an open heart for you and an open heart for all. It's my hope that this resonates with you, some way, somehow. That deep within the soft, central core of your being, you know these words are directly meant for you. That the message is exactly what you need to hear. That it stirs you and awakens you. That it cracks open your shell.

It is my hope you read this not only from cover to cover but that you return to passages, poems or chapters to re-read and re-think. I hope you have the time to pause and wonder so all the messages allow you to unfold. As you unfold, from beyond your shell, you will slowly reveal your own brilliant and majestic yolk. As you re-ignite and re-engage with *you*, you will miraculously find yourself connecting with others. It's in this place of connection to yourself, to your yolk, that you will find the answers you are looking for. And you will find that what you are searching for … finds you.

Absolute brilliance, power and awe happen when all our yolks connect. When we all live from this place of connection and love. This is when mountains are moved. This fuels profound change for all of humanity.

But let's start with the basics.

One beautiful yolk at a time.

INTRODUCTION

Fast track to your funeral. You see a room full of your friends and family. You feel a great sense of love in the room, love for you, the departed. Someone dear to you is delivering your eulogy. Tears are being shed, memories relived and smiles are interspersed with tears. Love engulfs the space and all in it.

And the words of the eulogy ... they describe your yolk, the best bits of you, the authentic parts of who you were, your essence, all the very best bits. Your kindness, your love, your generosity, your God-given talents and authentic qualities; the stories, the examples, the very core of you.

Some would call it your heart. Some would call it your soul, some your spirit. The religious might call it the God or godliness in you or of you. But I call it your yolk.

That bright, brilliantly coloured and soft, central core of you, the centre of all your loveliness, hidden – perhaps – behind your shell.

I believe that discovering, loving and expressing your yolk is the cornerstone of living a happy and fulfilled life and the doorway to meaningful connections with others. Self-love must come first; revealing your yolk, braving vulnerability and finding courage, a close second. Beneath the shell is where the true magic lies.

So, who am I to write this book, to spread this message? I am nobody special, but equally, I am special enough. I am enough, and I believe wholeheartedly in this message.

I believe it's a message for us all as teachers, students, parents, adults, children young and old. I believe we are all inextricably connected, and because of this the message resonates at our deep, connected core. I believe this is a tangible and simple way to teach us how to find our true selves.

There are many books and teachings about this, but the concepts are often hard to grasp. The language can be complex, spiritual and difficult to absorb. The information overload causes some to disconnect. How are we to find our way forward and find a path inward if we don't understand how to start looking? How do we even decide to look if there is no catalyst or calling to do so? How do we get ourselves out of the mess and back on course when we haven't even acknowledged we are off course?

How can we proceed?

We are at a major crossroad of humanity. We are all being urged to find a greater meaning to life and how we live the gift that's been given to us.

Too many of us waste this gift by just going through the motions, day after day. It's an autopilot way of existing. There's little meaning and limited joy. There's no time for creativity, there's no freedom or flexibility, and there is no roadmap to find our way out. So, we aimlessly move through life without tapping into all that it has to offer. I believe there's a better way, and I hope that by following the thread woven through this book, you will find it.

This book aims not to confuse you with complex spiritual concepts and religious undertones. It won't take you so deep that you are struggling for air. It won't exclude you, patronise you or criticise you. It won't preach to you like a religion. It aims to teach you through simple metaphors and examples. It wants to connect with you as you connect with yourself. It's like mother earth tucking you – the child – into bed and reading a story with a message just for you. It's like the loving advice from your best friend or close confidant. It has only your best interests at heart. There is no agenda, just a helping hand.

INTRODUCTION

This book teaches you three easy steps:

1. Love your yolk.
2. Express your yolk.
3. Cultivate your yolk.

Then you will find yourself. You will connect with *you*. Then, only then, will you move forward. When you connect within, you open the doorway to connect to everything and everyone, in this life and in the afterlife. Yes, death is no barrier to connection. Meaningful connections forged in this life continue after death.

This book is full of stories illustrating this magic.

Why should you put your trust in me? I am a mother, a daughter, a sister, a wife, a Physiotherapist, a Pilates Instructor, a meditator, a medium, an Intuitive Mentor, a friend, a teacher and a student. Wearing all of these hats and playing and loving all of these roles means I place great value on my message in the words of this book.

I am a writer, writing for you *and* me; I am one voice. But I am also the voice of many who have gone before me. I'm writing for them as much as for me, and they want me to write this for us all.

I believe this book's merit is in what it provides; help and hope, in equal measure. I believe life gives us all the ability to spread a message and share our wisdom, no matter where that wisdom is found. I believe the only thing that holds us back is fear; fear of judgement, fear of vulnerability, fear of cracking open the shell and exposing our yolks.

Fear keeps us small inside our shells. Love opens us up to reveal our yolks.

So, in the pages of this book I expose my vulnerable yolk in all its authenticity and glory. I do this in the hope you will see this is the way forward for you, and for all of us. The way forward is open and limitless if you are prepared to venture forth, knowing you will see many twists and turns on your path, and receive many lessons along the road to self-discovery. The key is not to let fear steer you off course.

Once you tap into your own intrinsic majesty embedded in your perfect yolk, you sail forward with the breeze upon your back. You follow your own path. You write your own story. What you seek is already within, just waiting to be birthed. Once you awaken to this reality your life begins to change.

You start on your own path by loving your yolk; you take every opportunity to express its glory and individuality. You partake in daily practices to cultivate its growth, and you evolve. You trust in the unknown and let your yolk guide you forward to experience the fullness of life that awaits you.

I hope you are prepared to venture on this journey. If you can walk with me to the end of the book, you will discover the magic of the everlasting yolk. The miraculous stories will illustrate the potential you have to be guided by spirit as you walk your way through life; guided by forces which are far greater than any one individual; forces which govern the natural order of everything and everyone.

If you allow me to chip away my own shell as I write, you will discover the majestic yolk of this book towards the end, as it's a gentle and delicate reveal of both my yolk and the heart of the book. Allow us to slowly unfold together and trust that we will.

But first, allow me to reveal a small piece of the magic; allow me to introduce the story of Bill, my father in law, who was the true inspiration for this book. In this story I show you how my own

INTRODUCTION

journey of loving, expressing and cultivating my own yolk opened the door to connection, to spirit, to my loved ones who had passed on. It shows you a glimpse of the wonder and magic of connection, and of the synchronicities in play that are calling us to tap into our yolks in order to evolve.

If it can happen to me and for me, it can happen for you. This is my greatest hope.

The story of Bill

My father in law, Bill, passed away in December 1997. He was diagnosed with cancer only nine months before his passing.

My husband and his father were very close. My husband Mark was Bill's only son. They worked in business together, and Bill was both his father and mentor. Mark took his father's passing particularly hard.

I have always felt that Bill died before he was ready, that his illness took a hold and did not afford him the time to put things in order as he would have liked. I therefore always had a sense that Bill remained close in spirit after his passing, as if to see us through the first few years without his physical presence.

I would describe Bill's yolk as very honourable and wise, gently guiding and thoughtful, insightful, measured and fair. He was dignified, respected, humorous, loving, generous and devoted.

A few days after his passing, my husband and I went to visit the cemetery where Bill had been buried. At the time we had a 10-month-old baby named Joshua. The cemetery was empty at this early hour and was quiet and still. The grass was wet with dew, and many of the graves were decorated with carefully arranged flowers. We walked gently in the spaces between the flowers to stop at the mound of disturbed earth where Bill's body had been laid to rest.

Quietly my husband knelt down at his father's grave while I put our baby boy down on the grass to crawl around and explore. Mark gently planted a kiss to his fingertips and pressed his fingers to the earth. As he did this, in his thoughts he explained to his father that he was feeling lost without him and could he please give him a sign that he was still with him.

Bill and Mark followed an AFL football team for which the mascot is a magpie. They both had a love of their team and shared this connection. My husband was planning for his young son to follow the same team too. At that very second three majestic magpies appeared, interrupting the stillness and silence. They swooped low, directly above our heads, and matched their swift movement with noisy squawks.

At that instant I said to my boy, 'Look Joshua, Grandpa has sent the magpies to show us he is still watching over.' As my beautiful boy looked skyward to watch the magpies fly above, my husband looked at me with complete wonder and awe. He took a few silent moments to process what had transpired, and then we silently wandered back to our car to put the baby in his car seat. When in the car, Mark turned to me and said, 'Do you know that at the exact moment you said about Dad sending the magpies, I had just asked him for a sign that he was with us?'

We stared at each other, absorbing what had just transpired, and then we both broke into the biggest smiles. We knew it was a clear sign of connection from Bill. We both felt a deep sense of knowing; not knowing *how*, not knowing *why*, but still knowing with unwavering certainty. It was a moment in which time stood still, in order for the wonder and awe to permeate.

INTRODUCTION

There are no words to do justice to the absolute majesty of that moment. The three magpies arrived at that precise moment in time, to deliver a message of hope and faith. The timing was perfect, the setting quiet and still, the meaning not lost on a son deeply grieving his father and a daughter in law wanting to provide him comfort.

We both felt an immense sense of comfort that Bill was still present and watching over. We were still connected, even after his death. It is still to this day so imprinted in our memories and brings us both such a feeling of peace and comfort.

Since that day the magpie has become Bill's calling card, and it serves as a constant and unwavering reminder that connection remains unbroken by death; that bonds forged in our lifetimes live on.

We, as a family, see and hear a magpie's call at different times and always feel it is Bill making his presence known. Whether it's a birthday or other special occasion, we often see a magpie and always feel it is a sign from Bill. We now have four children, three of whom were born after Bill's passing, yet all of them have a connection to him through the magpie. It keeps his memory alive.

During his years approaching retirement, Bill and his wife purchased a block of land at Sorrento on the Mornington Peninsula. They built a holiday home where we as a family spent many wonderful times. A few years after his passing our family spent one weekend there. We were strolling through the main street past a bookshop. As we passed, I had a very unusual but definite feeling I was supposed to go into the store and buy a particular book.

I knew it was Bill encouraging me, almost *urging* me to do so. I said to my husband that Bill was asking me to buy a particular book and I was going into the store to do so. I walked into the shop not really knowing what book I was looking for. But in an instant I saw it; the very book I knew I must purchase and read. It was called *Send Me Someone: A true love story of love here and hereafter* by Diana von Welanetz Wentworth. This book was about a man who dies of cancer but makes it very apparent he is still present in his wife's life. It was about communication from the other side. I knew without any doubt this was the book Bill was leading me to buy.

I read this book with wonder and realised I was not alone. That many of us have clear, undeniable signs our departed loved ones are still with us. Incredibly, this book also had many references to birds being the messengers or signs of a departed one.

It was a lightbulb moment for me. I knew what I had always felt, always sensed was correct. I knew I was not alone, that others felt how I did, and miraculous signs presented to them as well.

One day I was in the laundry folding washing and pondering the significance of the book and what it might mean for me personally. I knew I had received similar signs from many who had passed on but I did not really talk about it to anyone. I knew deep within that connections continued, and death was no barrier to receiving guidance and love from loved ones. I had always felt this, always known this truth. But I lacked the courage to tell people about it, at the risk of being judged.

As I looked out the small laundry window and into the garden, I impulsively sent out a challenge to my father in law. I said, 'Okay Bill, I know you sent me the magpies, and others have sent me lots of signs too. Am I supposed to write a book about them? If so, send me a bird sign right here, right now.'

INTRODUCTION

I was challenging him to give me some clarity, proving to me what I was intuitively feeling inside was what I was being guided to do.

Instantly I heard the loud cries of several birds, so loud and present I was startled. I jumped in response to the noise. Yet ... there was not a bird to be seen out the window. I walked slowly out of the laundry and into the living room, where my husband was watching television. On the screen were hundreds of loud, squawking birds. I was in shock. My husband turned to see me standing there in bewilderment, and said, 'You look like you've just seen a ghost.'

I stood transfixed, trying to process what had just unfolded. I knew with unwavering clarity I was meant to write a book about these signs. I knew what I was being nudged to do. I knew that it was crucial for all of us to understand about the power of connection, and to learn how to see the signs. I knew I had a small part to play in helping to teach others how to connect in order to receive guidance from loved ones in spirit.

So, this is my story. It's taken me 15 years of procrastination, denial and fear to reach this point. I have pretended not to believe the signs, dismissed them, ignored them, turned a blind eye. In doing so I have felt I've been ignoring a deeper part of myself which needed to be seen and heard.

I now realise I have been hiding within my own shell of fear.

It's taken me 15 years of healing myself from the inside out to finally have the courage to write this book. The most amazing part of this whole story is that in applying my own code, my own road-map of loving, expressing and cultivating my yolk, I have been able to birth this book.

I am the product of my own work. I have lived and breathed every lesson, every step, every example, every story. It's no surprise the bird references led me to a book entitled *Yolk*. Once I embraced my story and cracked open my shell of fear, I came to the realisation that millions of us have our own stories; miraculous and uplifting stories of the ongoing love and presence of a loved one.

So many of us are enormously comforted by these stories, and are comforted by the stories of others. Who am I to stand in the way of comfort? Who am I to stay small and safe and hidden and prevent you from being comforted by these stories of hope?

My mediumship and intuitive skills help me to understand that our departed loved ones need and want us to learn about connection. They *want* us to know they are still present, just in a different form. They say connecting with us helps them. It helps them in their spiritual journey.

I don't quite understand all the intricacies, but I know with absolute clarity our departed loved ones want their presence to be felt. They are as alive and present as our memories of them are. If we think of, talk about and remember them, they are more present.

INTRODUCTION

If our thoughts shape our reality, then keeping our thoughts of our loved ones in the present keeps them present with us.

It's as if the pages of this book are not only to help me tell my story, but to help them too, so we are all aware of the potential, and we can all look for the signs and, most importantly, we can all be granted the peace and comfort of knowing they are still present.

Before I reveal the yolk of this book and all these magical stories, let us chip away our shells together, step by step. Let me help you first to love *your* yolk; let me show you how to express it; let me teach you how to cultivate it so you are living in alignment with your truth. Then, let me reveal more of these stories to give you hope; hope for this life and the next, so you too can find connection in this life and beyond.

But first, I need to reveal a little of my own yolk.

Fear keeps us small
inside our shells.
Love opens us up to
reveal our yolks.

BERNADETTE SOMERS

1. Discovering my yolk

THEY SAY THAT writers are compelled to write about something they themselves need to learn, and so it is with me. This book has helped me understand myself more and learn about my own yolk. It has helped me find my voice. The process of writing has chipped away my shell. This book has helped me to tap into *me*; it has taught me to show up for *me*; it has made me stretch and it has made me grow as a person.

I believe many people write as they believe they have a message that will help others, but I believe the writing must first and foremost help the writer. This book has helped me to heal and has changed me for the better. It has given me the courage to share my voice so I can help others. It has taught me to get out of my own way, move out of my shadow and stand proudly in my light. It has also taught me how to have more self-love.

If you can understand how I have slowly achieved this, how I have journeyed to this point, how this roadmap has helped me, it will help *you* chip away at *your* shell. So, I'm going to share my journey with you.

When I was a young child I was always described as quiet and shy. I was the middle child of seven children, and was part of an extremely loving, fun family. I believe that, in some way, I signed up for this family, like it was my soul contract. I now think it was part of my life challenge to find my voice.

When I was five years old and in my first year of school, my prep teacher, Sister Helena, chose me to give the opening speech at the school's end-of-year concert. My mother was worried I was too shy to do this, and told my teacher. However, Sister Helena was adamant I was the right girl for the role.

The auditorium was full with people when I went onto the stage, and I stepped up onto a small wooden step to bring me up to the height of the microphone. I faced the audience, spoke clearly and confidently, and gave the speech. My teacher was pleased, and was reassured that her decision to select me was correct.

This moment is one of my clearest memories of growing up, and now, after writing this book, I see its significance. It was the beginning of me finding my voice, of connecting with others as an individual. I realise now that life was ready to play ball; and I was a child of an age that was ready to play. Life presented me with the opportunity to express the potential of my yolk.

Life is always providing us with opportunities for growth and experiences from which to learn. When we are young, we care less about judgement and we are more willing to seize opportunities. Unfortunately, as we get older, we can increasingly let our shells of fear stand in our way. I drew on that memory to give me the courage to write this book. It inspires me to realise we all have the potential to do things others may not expect of us, that stretch us and push us to become who we are meant to be.

Another defining memory of my younger life is when I was 10 years old. I was waiting at the school bus stop to catch the bus home and found myself in the midst of four older boys taunting and mocking a younger girl. They were teasing and laughing at her, and I witnessed bullying for the first time. Everyone at the bus stop watched silently but no-one tried to intervene.

Without warning, I raised my voice and told the boys to stop. I then calmly proceeded to tell them that 'they wouldn't do that to God, so they shouldn't do that to her'. Everyone fell silent and was stunned – most of all me. I couldn't believe I had given a religious lesson to this bunch of bullies. One of the boys made a comment, but essentially my words made them stop.

I don't know where exactly I got the strength to say what I said, but I feel it came from deep within, from my yolk. I felt true empathy for the defenceless girl, and I found my voice to defend her. I braved vulnerability and expressed myself and what I wanted to do; to help and to care. I didn't second guess myself or procrastinate; I just did what I knew was right.

I showed up. I showed up for that girl, and I showed up for me. That was indeed the lesson of it all. For many years after, I was so embarrassed about the bus stop incident. But now I look back and realise it was just another opportunity for me to find my voice.

I'm now very proud of that young, brave 10-year-old girl. I realise that my individual actions on that day were not about myself, but about others. I now understand that life always works in our favour when we are trying to be of service to others. Connection is the fundamental link; we will be supported in our lives when our actions are for the greater good of all.

WEARING THE SHOES

Now with the wisdom of my years I can identify that I am an empath; I am really sensitive to what others around me are feeling. I tend to feel that sense of connection to others quite strongly.

Empathy is very different from showing sympathy. As an analogy, if someone is wearing very uncomfortable shoes which are crippling their feet, one could look at them and feel sympathy for them but feel very glad they are not wearing the shoes. For an empath, *they wear the shoes as well.* They wear the shoes for the other person. They feel it. I have always 'worn the shoes' for anyone who has experienced loss; loss of a loved one, loss of a pregnancy, loss of a baby. I feel their loss quite deeply. I just have no other option than to feel it.

I now realise that these qualities of my own yolk are meant to be expressed; that empathy and compassion benefit others; they are for the greater good. When I brave vulnerability and express them, I form connections with others, as life encourages the expression of all qualities that facilitate connection.

As an empath it is especially difficult to cope with death and loss. My first experience of losing a loved one and experiencing death was with my grandfather, Robert – or Bob, as he was usually called. I was eighteen at the time and unfamiliar with grief. Bob died from heart complications arising from emphysema. I visited him in hospital the day before his passing, and was unaware and unprepared that this would be the final time I saw him.

After Papa had passed away, the family all went to my Nana's house. It was as if someone had entered their home and shifted the furniture around, it felt so out of place being in the home without him.

I was feeling such empathy for my Nan that I decided to pen a letter to her. The words of the letter were my attempt to reproduce the most beautiful poem I had ever read. It is entitled *Death is Nothing at All*, by Henry Scott Holland.

Death is Nothing at All

I have only slipped away to the next room.
I am I and you are you.
Whatever we were to each other
That, we still are.
Call me by my old familiar name,
Speak to me in the easy way
which you always used
Put no difference into your tone,
Wear no forced air of solemnity or sorrow.

Laugh as we always laughed
at the little jokes we enjoyed together
Play, smile, think of me Pray for me
Let my name be ever the household word
that it always was.
Let it be spoken without effect.
Without the trace of a shadow on it.

Life means all that it ever meant.
It is the same that it ever was.

> There is absolute unbroken continuity.
> Why should I be out of mind?
> because I am out of sight?
> I am but waiting for you.
> For an interval.
> Somewhere. Very near.
> Just around the corner.
>
> **HENRY SCOTT HOLLAND**

The first time I read this poem I knew it was truth. I knew with unwavering certainty that there was unbroken continuity. It spoke to the very depths of me, and gave me the faith to understand death and loss in a completely different way. It felt as if it ignited the spark within me to find my voice, and to eventually write this book. I felt I had an opportunity to show others how to cope with loss. I had found my way, as an empath, to deal with loss, and now I had to show others the same path to help them heal.

So, I wrote similar words to my grandmother, and slipped my secret letter under her pillow, so that when she was ready for sleep she could read it and be comforted. I knew when she was alone and reflective, she would most feel his loss. This was my gift to Nan. Our little secret.

It was also my first and most important piece of writing. I was finding my voice and putting it in words, and trying to help and heal with those words. I was helping and healing myself as much as I was trying to help my Nana. I was tapping into me, bringing forth what was within, with love front and centre.

I didn't know it at the time, but I was expressing my yolk.

The next day my parents pulled me aside to tell me Nana had told them of my letter. Suddenly I felt embarrassed and vulnerable. But my father said to me that it showed I had depth, and he thought it was a lovely gesture.

I now look back at this first attempt at writing and see many parallels with writing my book. As you can see, the motives are the same; I want to help and I want to connect.

NOT AN EASY RIDE

I realise that living in alignment with my yolk, my truth, is not an easy ride. It's sometimes a stretch. But to stay safe is to stay small. To sit in the flow is to sit in the space between comfort and slight discomfort in order to stretch and grow. I know this now.

I have to tap in, show up and stretch. The three steps to this are:

1. love
2. express
3. cultivate.

So, this book is my example of following my own roadmap, the one I share with you in these pages. It's my gift to myself and to you, in equal measure.

Sometimes it's hard to show up for ourselves and stretch. But we must listen to the inner calling; we must find the courage, because showing up and expressing ourselves fosters connection.

In my life I have faced many opportunities to stretch. For example, I have found my voice to sing in a band. I have always felt that singing was the creative expression of my yolk. Something I was meant to do to bring me joy. Once I learnt to step out of my own way and make fear my friend, I learnt to sing in front of an audience and express my yolk.

Now when I sing, it feeds my soul, and I don't care anywhere near as much about judgement. It feels so damn good to tap into the creativity of my yolk. It feels right, and it will always feel like it stretches me. It allows me to sit between comfort and discomfort in order to grow.

ARE YOU READY TO PLAY?

So now I understand the process; that life is looking to play ball. You have to be ready to catch it, or it will land with someone else. I caught the ball – I wrote this book. So, I ask you: are *you* ready to play ball? More importantly, are you ready to *catch it*?

I want you to realise it is the one ball that we all play with; a ball which services us all equally in this big game of life. A ball is meant to be thrown between people, and played with together. That is how life works. Life will always assist us to play together, for mutual benefit, for connection. So, if we open up to connection, we open up to life. This is the cornerstone of my message, delivered in this book and through this unique roadmap.

It is my hope that this book has opened your arms so you are ready to play and ready to catch.

Writing this book has been a joy. I have now discovered that when you follow your joy, it can bring joy to others. I know many a book sits on a shelf in a library never to be opened and brought to life. My hope is this book has opened your arms and fallen into your hands for a reason; into safe hands.

My hope is this book speaks directly to you – to your yolk – and that it helps you and heals you, as it did me. And I hope your hands will enable it to fall into others' hands to continue to spread the message, so you too can help and connect with others, so you join in this ripple effect, and together we can grow this ripple into a wave to serve others. This is my hope, and I leave my hope in your hands.

So, now I have revealed a little of my own yolk, let me show you how to love yours in the following chapters.

Love is Mine

My origin and destination
My anchor to the shore
Love embraces and delivers me
To where I need no more

Than the touch of newborn skin
Divine guidance of a soul
A flower's purest scent
No pain, no earthly toll

My intuition and my wisdom
My sense of what is right
Sweet warmth of all embraces
The whisper still of night

I know my own existence
Serves a purpose set in time
I live and breathe, heal and renew
For love, true love is mine

BERNADETTE SOMERS

2. Loving your yolk

WE ARE BORN a blank canvas, an unadulterated perfect and pure yolk. We are born into this world free of conditioning, limiting beliefs, pain or negativity. We are beautifully open and pure, full of loving potential and limitless possibility. Our needs are hopefully met by loving and obliging parents or caregivers. The world is our oyster.

OUR SHELLS

We start life with an unblemished yolk full of promise and potential, without the confines of a shell. As we develop and grow, we begin to form our thoughts and create our own beliefs based on our environment, our circumstances and the people who surround us. Over time, we develop our shells, our walls, our armour.

We take on the beliefs of others as our own. We learn self-limiting beliefs about ourselves, our abilities, our attributes, our skillsets. We learn about the perceived limitations of our gender, our age and our appearance. We take on limiting beliefs from our parents, teachers and role models in our community and inner circle. When we're still developing, we don't have the wisdom to challenge these limiting beliefs. We don't have the life experience. We simply accept what we are told. We accept it as truth. Slowly these beliefs and limits become our shell, and from inside this shell we stay small. We may never learn to break free in order to grow.

But beyond the constraints of our shell lies great possibility and potential. Breaking free from the constraints of our shell enables us to live a life of love not fear, to dare to dream, to challenge limiting beliefs, to be vulnerable and courageous.

To do this, we need to love our yolks. We need to have self-belief and self-worth. We need to honour what is inside us, our true authentic essence. It's with this love that we can step forward to live our truth.

Most successful people will tell you they have had many setbacks and roadblocks on their path to success. Most successful people have been equipped with enough self-belief to propel them forward along their path. With perseverance, they weather the storms and push on through difficult times. The light of self-belief shows them the way forward.

Loving our yolks gives us the self-belief to push forward. Breaking free from the confines of our shells enables us to live a life of love, not fear. It may be safe to stay tucked within the safety of our shells, but it is not tapping into the potential of our yolks.

SELF-LOVE

The most important message in this book is one of self-love, and that love is found beneath the shell. Self-love is the biggest gift we can give ourselves, for gift wrapped with the gift of self-love is self-worth. When we love ourselves, we improve our self-worth.

We all have just one life to lead, one chance at this game, and it is meant to be spent loving ourselves. We must be our own champion. Self-love is not a moral flaw, it's mandatory for good physical and mental health. It is also necessary to love ourselves so we can in turn love others.

Life flows with more ease and less resistance if we truly love ourselves. It is the medicine that makes us less needy of approval and validation from others. It helps us back ourselves and stand up for ourselves, our voice, our opinions.

When we are full of self-love, we simply don't need validation from anyone else.

'All we need is love' should really be 'all we need is self-love'. It ultimately must come first, for when we love ourselves wholeheartedly, we can then love others the same way. When we lack love for ourselves, we can't truly love others. When we lack love for ourselves, we find there is less love available for others. When we have self-love, we expand and open up; we become open hearted and we find it easier to find love for others.

This is the amazing ripple effect of loving our yolks. When we love our yolks, we are instantly equipped to find love in others. When we feel self-love and are in a happy place, we are positioned in the very place that enables us to see love outside of ourselves.

Self-love doesn't just mean loving the parts of us that we approve of and ignoring the other parts – it means loving ourselves wholeheartedly, loving *all* facets of us, the good and the bad, the yolk and the shell.

We can't reject parts of ourselves; we can't deny ourselves unconditional acceptance. This is how we get ourselves into difficulty. We have to acknowledge our own shortcomings and love ourselves regardless. We have to love all the colours of our rainbows. If we deny even a little part of ourselves, we cannot move onto the next stage of true expression. If we can't fully love ourselves, we hinder the process of connection.

We all have light and shade; we are all a mix of yin and yang, good and bad. No-one is perfect. Everyone has something they need to work on, improve or acknowledge. There is no shame in that. We have to love ourselves regardless.

Life is meant to be lived to its fullest. Opportunities are meant to be taken. Dreams are meant to be pursued. All of this living happens best with the support of self-love. If we really love ourselves and accept our flaws, we are better equipped to roll with the punches and take chances. We are less likely to beat ourselves up when we fail. We honour ourselves and our efforts.

Life is supposed to have its twists and turns, its ups and downs; that is the lesson of it. That's how we evolve. When we love ourselves, warts and all, we are less rattled by those twists and turns, less worried by the setbacks. Life provides us with our beautiful, untainted yolks bursting with potential and possibilities, so it can be birthed from that potential. Loving our yolks, really loving them unconditionally, enables us to really feel that potential as limitless.

When we live bringing our yolks to the forefront with self-love and acceptance, wonderful things unfold. That is how, where and why we make meaningful connections. Revealing our true selves means being vulnerable, which leaves us no other option than to be authentic. When we hide within our shells to avoid being vulnerable, others may disconnect from us. The yolks are like the magnet connecting us all together. But the magnet cannot function if shielded by the shells.

Think of all the times when you have formed meaningful connections with others; at school, at work, at play. Really getting to know someone involves getting a good glimpse of the core of who they are – all the parts that make them real and authentic, their vulnerabilities, their emotions, their passions.

Seeing others' vulnerabilities helps us to recognise our own and accept them too.

In accepting our own imperfections, we can become more accepting of others' imperfections. We realise we are all the same, all just trying to do our best at this thing called life. We learn that it's okay to drop our guards, to control less, to resist less and to allow more. To settle into that space in the present moment and just *be*; just be the best expression of our authentic and beautiful yolks.

That's authentic living and that's authentic loving. That should be in everyone's eulogies.

GOD IN THE YOLK

I have spent most of my life following a religious code. Yet I do not describe myself as religious. I wouldn't call myself spiritual either – instead I would reframe it and say that I am *full of spirit*. My spirit is within my yolk. It's a quality I possess, but it does not define me as religious or spiritual. It's an intrinsic part of me.

I had a Catholic upbringing. I was raised by wonderful parents in a very loving and supportive family. I was one of seven children. I was baptised as a baby. Our family went to church every Sunday morning, as we were taught to do. I attended both a Catholic primary school and secondary school. I celebrated Easter and Christmas and fasted during Lent.

My Catholic faith was always there, in the background, providing a basic moral framework for me personally and for my family. There were many rules and regulations that were expected to be followed. I was expected to make my first Reconciliation, Communion and Confirmation. I was expected to marry a male and do that in a church. I was expected to attend mass on a Sunday. I followed the rules and regulations without questioning their purpose or their validity.

I don't have any major regrets about my Catholic upbringing, but I do have very different views about religion now. I accept my religion provided me with a basic moral code to follow, but I don't think that necessarily needed to fall under the Catholic umbrella. And I now believe religions have the potential to create divisions between people who follow different customs and beliefs.

I'm not one to preach about religion; I am not forcing my ideas, theories or opinions on anyone. This book is not about religion, it is about connection.

I have come to my own individualised way of understanding how I can live my life with a basic moral framework. The fundamental link in all religions is God, but should be love. To choose love. To be love, to be loving. Love is found in our yolks. Love resides within; not in a church, not in a mosque, not in a synagogue. It is found within us. The bricks and mortar, the space of a church or temple is just a space to unite people.

Following a basic moral code means living a life of love, not fear. Knowing right from wrong, and loving and accepting everyone. Judging everyone by the goodness of their yolks and not the facades of their shells. Connecting with each other with empathy, compassion, non-judgement and acceptance.

Everything is found within. Everything is found in our yolks, the very place where love resides. Loving our yolks, loving our true authentic selves opens the doors for love to flow to others. It is that love that unifies us all. Love must come first. It is the answer.

I believe that if God exists, he exists in our yolks, that heaven is found within us.

We are here to learn that there is no separation, we are all connected, we all have our yolks, our inner core of beauty and purity, the expression of ourselves. We need to live our lives by finding the God or love that resides within and bringing it forth. Praying to different Gods creates separation. Finding God within our yolks connects us.

We all are born with pure, loving, compassionate qualities within. The words of the Catholic hymn spring to mind:

God is dwelling in my heart, he and I are one

God is found in the yolk.

I believe if we all live from a place where we find the 'God' in our yolks and live by expressing our yolks and bringing them to the forefront, we are living good lives, following a good moral code, decreasing separateness.

If God is love and love is within each and every one of us, then God is in our yolks.

If you believe in a God, he is within.

If you believe in love, it is within.

All is within.

If love never dies, then our yolks never die; love lives on, ever present. My 'religion' is to bring the qualities of my yolk to the forefront. To choose love over fear. To lead with my yolk.

No matter what God you believe in, his common denominator is love. And if you don't believe in a God then believe in love. You can't denounce love.

The truth of who we are is in our yolks, our inner core or essence. It is where the truth lies. It is beyond our bodies, beyond our shells. Within the yolk lies all the insight, all the information, all the access codes to open up to a happy life. It's all there just waiting to be accessed.

Now, some might say this all still sounds a bit spiritual. But I think spirituality is defined as the study of oneself and what is within. We are here to learn there is no separation or division, that we are all connected to what we are looking for, that we are what we seek.

Crack open the shell and see the yolk; see the deepest part of who we are. Look within, not outside for the answer, the religious code by which to abide. Find the love within the yolk and bring it forward. Connect the dots by connecting the yolks.

Many people connect religion to spirituality and feel this defines them as having a faith. Many are unsure about their faith and about God. There are just too many unanswered questions.

But if we use the word 'yolk', perhaps it's easier to relate. It might help to make more sense. It has no religious undertone, nor is it referring to anything deeply spiritual. It is just an analogy which refers to what's beneath the shell. Something that defines us and represents us. Something that is uniquely *ours*. Something deep and meaningful, authentic and real.

I wholeheartedly believe every living individual feels a connection to something deep inside of them, that space, that place within, that is pure and loving, that defines them as a loving, unique and authentic being. That at our very core we are all the same, all connected. It's our life force, our centre, our essence. It's the pivotal point of who we are and why we are here. It's the feeling inside that tells us we are all part of a grander plan, a greater calling.

By learning to really acknowledge our yolks, by tuning into them, they can be our compass. They can steer us in the right direction and navigate us forward towards happiness and contentment. They can open us up to allowing things to unfold as they are meant to, and show us the lessons to learn along the way. They can help us to stop resisting, controlling and orchestrating everything and just trust the direction we are being steered in.

As an example of love and a life spent loving, let me share the story of Clare, a devoted mother who still loved and guided her daughter from the other side, transcending countries and dimensions.

The story of Clare

My friend, who lives in Canada, lost her mother Clare to cancer several years ago.

Clare was a lovely lady, sure footed and grounded, with a great sense of humour. She was the loving sister of Bill, my father in law. She was the invisible thread that united them all together; the matriarch of a close-knit and loving family.

Clare always spoke her word and spoke the truth. She did not beat around the bush. Her yolk was loyal, devoted and steadfast. She was reliable, unwavering and wise; a great friend and respected individual. She faced her illness and all the challenges in her life with a dignified acceptance and grace. Her passing left a great void in the life of her husband and four children.

My friend called me one day after her mother had passed. We didn't speak on a regular basis but were good friends separated by distance. Her call was a pleasant surprise.

She had been thinking about her mother and wanted guidance on a business venture she was contemplating. She admitted she struggled with the concept of connection with spirit, yet really yearned for a connection with her mother.

Her call to me was no coincidence. It was setting the tone and triggering a series of events that would enable Clare to respond to her daughter's plea for guidance. I was the conduit for this to occur.

That day while meditating, Clare came to me with a message for her daughter. She told me life delivers the opportunities you are meant to pursue. She said she had been trying to connect with her daughter, and went on to convey a very beautiful and private message for my friend. This message would give her the guidance she was searching for.

I asked Clare to provide me with a sign to validate the message to her daughter and assist her to trust in its validity. She showed me an image of an unusual and beautiful bird native to British Columbia. She said her daughter would know this particular bird with a black face, black fan on its head, and coloured blue and purple. Clare showed me an image of the bird hopping around the back yard of her daughter's home and venturing very close to the back window. She said this particular bird could be her sign for her daughter to connect with her.

I immediately searched online for birds native to British Columbia, and to my amazement the first picture shown was a blue jay. It was exactly as Clare had shown, with a black face and fan on its head.

I called my friend to pass on Clare's message and tell her about the blue jay. She was also amazed, and told me she had many blue jays visit her back garden.

She said she had one in particular come in ever so close to the back window, and she and her husband had thought it was unusual. She told her daughter the story and she too had seen a blue Jay come right up to the window, looking in at her when she was home alone. My friend described how the blue jays hopped around her garden just as Clare had shown me. We both were truly amazed by the sign Clare had given to illustrate her ongoing presence and guidance.

Clare's maternal love still anchored her to her family despite her passing. The loving, steadfast and loyal qualities of her yolk were still present.

This was another shining example of how the essence of a person stays with them in the afterlife. How the absolute hallmarks of their character, their heart and their soul live on. The yolk is eternal, eternally ours and eternally loved by those who truly love us.

My connection with spirit and all the everlasting yolks has opened my eyes to one big reality, which is that love is the answer. Once we open ourselves to love and love ourselves, love our yolks, all will fall into place. Once we show love to ourselves, the doors of flow open up where all is revealed and received. Once we truly love our yolks, we find our true selves. We become in sync and in flow. We can reside in the place where all things unfold as they are meant to, where we feel aligned, where all is true. We can surrender all worries and become fearless. We can live our lives with bravery and courage. We can know our truths and live them. We no longer have to water ourselves down to blend and please. We can be our authentic selves so we can finish what we have set out to do in this life's path.

Loving our yolks is the first step.

THE BOARD GAME OF LIFE

Life is like a board game. When we roll the dice and move forward a few places on our board, we have to then take stock in our new position. There is a reason and purpose to stopping there, why the numbers fell that way. When we learn the reason, we can roll the dice again, move forward and keep playing the game, keep evolving. But when we don't learn the lessons, we become stuck; there is no progress.

Failing to learn equates to failing to move forward. We can move forward once we learn the lessons at each stop. Every roll of the dice takes us to where we next need to go to learn and grow – once we trust the dice.

Once we trust the process, we allow the dice to choose the next stop and know that there is a purpose and reason behind it. We get to sit in that contented space of just trusting the board game, allowing the game to unfold, and knowing we will all eventually make it to the end of our games enriched by the experience and all the lessons learned. That's how we grow, how we evolve; that is the ride, that is the whole purpose. That's what we are all here for.

Every one of us has unique rolls of the dice, but we are all playing the same universal board game, all joined, all connected. There are no wrong moves, as every step is progress. We are all heading to the same place. The key is to *enjoy* the game, take our time, absorb every moment, every stop, every roll. It is in that present state that we truly absorb the lessons.

The board game is not one of snakes and ladders. There is no quick way up a ladder to the end of the game. And even if we could do that, we would short-change ourselves of all the wisdom we accrue while travelling the board. We are *meant* to travel the whole board. That's experience.

When we love our yolks, love ourselves wholeheartedly, we can enjoy the game, go with the flow and roll with the punches. We don't tend to over-analyse or second guess ourselves as much. We are able to sit more in a space of flow and ease because everything feels underpinned by a strong sense of self-love and acceptance.

We all know people who play the victim, who blame the dice for rolling and delivering them to a place or circumstance they did not want or plan on. They do not want to take any responsibility; they use blame as their defence or their weapon. They fail to see the lesson that needs to be learnt at that particular spot on the board. They have a 'why me?' mentality and find it difficult to move forward.

They can become stuck. They are not listening in the silence to the truth of the situation; they are not seeing it with clarity and self-love to accept responsibility, admit wrong, forgive themselves and move forward. Often there is an underlying unhappiness which acts as a catalyst for this reaction and behaviour.

Stopping at the first roadblock and blaming others will not allow progress. That's how and why people stagnate, how they become entangled in their own victim story. They refuse to let go of their story because it means they must go inward. They must connect with their yolk with compassion, forgiveness and love. They must crack open the shell, release the fear, the anger, the hurt, and whatever else is holding them back.

If we look inward we can see we are all having a human experience, trying to play our best board game and learning as we go. That is the journey, and we all need the journey to evolve.

With the connection of our human experience, we realise we all have roadblocks, we all have setbacks; we all are destined to experience the set of experiences that enable us to evolve. That is the whole point of living a life; it's a journey with twists and turns.

No-one's life is without roadblocks. Everyone has their 'stuff' to work through and navigate around. Often people are just doing the best they can with what they have. Life is not a walk in the park; if it was there would be nothing to learn, no wisdom to gain, nowhere to progress to, no evolution. If we all change our mindsets to see setbacks and roadblocks as opportunities from which to learn, we might be less likely to repeat a mistake; we might learn from it and move forward on the board.

WE ARE EXACTLY WHERE WE ARE MEANT TO BE

If we see life in this manner and we trust in the process, we can let go of fear and control. We have the opportunity to live life with presence, enjoying the moments as they happen, being in the moment, being engaged and centred. I believe happiness is found in that space; it's found in the moment of realising that *we are exactly where we are meant to be*. This awareness can free us from needing to control every roll of the dice. Trust can allow us to go with the natural flow of life, to roll with the punches, to enjoy the ride.

There are times when many of us will question the fairness of the game, why some will suffer and fall countless times along the way. Why some people seem to have more pain, more trauma, more sadness, more setbacks. Why some move forward relatively easily, yet some deal with hardships and roadblocks every step of the way.

What – we ask – is the lesson in that? For the family of a loved one who dies in an accident, for victims of abuse, for the sick and the poor. How do we make sense of these circumstances, these examples of human suffering? It seems unfair and unbalanced. How do we understand why some people seem to be getting so many lessons to learn on their board game?

The only truth in all of this is that despite challenges, loss and suffering, we will never lose our yolks. Time may wither us, circumstances and hardships may deplete us, sadness may stunt us, illness may cripple us, but our yolks remain untainted.

Our yolks are untouchable, always pure and perfect. They cannot be tarnished by life's toil; they remain intact and inside. They are our treasured possessions. We can always tune into them, look deeply within and know they will always be the same. Everlasting.

We can find strength from that knowing. We can realise that no matter what life throws at us we will always have our yolks and nothing can take them from us. The solace found in this can help us when the dice seems to continually roll against us. It is our hope when all hope seems lost; it is our certainty when all seems uncertain.

If we sit in silence and truly reflect, we may find some comfort from this. No matter what life throws at us along the way, we were born with our big, beautiful yolks, and we get to leave with them too. They are untainted and unblemished, no matter what we do or what life does to us.

I have an unwavering belief that we are all part of a collective process, all spokes in a big wheel, all cylinders in a big engine that propels us forward collectively. I believe everything that happens, every person we meet, every occurrence has its place on our board game of life.

When we open up to this reality, many more opportunities present. We connect with likeminded people; we find ourselves at the right places at the right time. A job opportunity presents itself, a dream home becomes available for sale, a business opportunity unfolds.

All occurrences are like musical notes that create a beautiful symphony. Yet we can't hear the music until the piece has evolved. Every experience, every occurrence is meant to shape us into who we are meant to be and illustrate what we are meant to learn.

Some of us have reality check moments or character defining moments that make us reflect and re-evaluate everything. I think that those moments are part of the plan, notes in our symphony. Looking at them in the present can make them hard to accept; when we experience hardship, when we experience grief or loss. It seems unfair or unjust. That's because all we have available to us is the ability to view it from our standpoint. We can't see the bigger picture. We can't hear the complete symphony. We can't project to the future and look back at it with clarity. So, our only option is to trust.

It's like following the thread; not really knowing how and when things will pan out but holding that thread and trusting in the process.

Trust gives us the clarity to realise we don't always have to lead, we will also be led. There are greater forces at play that are working in our favour and will assist us, if we trust the bigger picture. We can never make a wrong choice, as every choice is right. Everything has its place, everything has its purpose. Everything is working out exactly as it's meant to and will deliver us to the end point exactly as it should.

I truly believe that when we adhere to this code of living, *everything* changes. Synchronicities occur, opportunities present, life starts to flow in its own natural rhythm. It becomes our path of least resistance.

BYPASSING THE WHITE

Sometimes it is in the darkness that we find the yolk. The defining moments, the reality checks, the wake-up calls. Often it is those very moments that break through our shells.

There are only two options from those moments:

- to stay broken; or
- to access the exposed yolk.

Those moments of adversity and struggle, of loss and heartache, provide us with the opportunity to see our yolks through the fractures. The fractures that have occurred through no fault of our own. The way the dice rolled, the circumstances that presented. The fractures in the shell give us two options: to sink or swim, to move forward or remain stuck, to heal or wither.

When we are broken, there is a small glimpse of solace in that through the cracks, we see our yolks. We see our depth, our love, our hopes and our resilience. We see we can be more than we think; stronger, braver. We can push on and push through.

Sometimes it's *only* in those very moments when we are stripped bare that we can find the strength to rise again.

But other times, it may feel like a struggle. There are times where uncovering and discovering the yolk just seems too hard. There are times when some find that the yolk is surrounded by a thick, dense and impenetrable white. There is a disconnect. It just doesn't feel like there is a way to tap in.

For those who cannot find their yolks, who feel their yolks have never been encouraged or validated, the *yolk* may feel like a *yoke*. A *yoke* is a heavy wooden beam attached over the necks of two animals to the plough they are to pull. The energetic frequency of this word *yoke* is in complete contrast to the inner gold of the word *yolk*.

But for some with disease and illness, particularly mental illness, that may be how it feels; a burden, a heavy weight. Despite how hard they try they can't reach the inner light of their yolks.

Mental illness, anxiety and depression are conditions so complex and complicated. They can hinder the ability to feel connected and anchored. They can separate some from the yolk's true identity and purpose. They can shield some from their yolks like a dense, stifling layer of white, preventing any access.

Depression might be a mix of physical, emotional and spiritual components. Disease and dis-ease are complicated and multifaceted. There may be hormonal, situational, chemical and nutritional factors at play. The journey navigating depression, anxiety and mental illness can be a long one. In the worst of cases, mental illness can lead to suicide.

For others, the white stands in the way of finding self-love. Some judge themselves harshly or punish themselves for every mistake they make. Others numb their pain with addiction and medication. Some feel disconnected, isolated and unable to find joy. Others feel a wall of negativity has shadowed their light.

How do they get past the white? How can they find a way in? How can they reach the yolk? And even if they *are* to reach it, how are they going to love what's there?

In discussing how to love your yolk and trying the Yolk Practices at the end of each chapter, I hope people who are suffering or having a difficult time can find relief. There is no quick fix and no single solution. But many people find comfort in putting this code and these practices in place. I am not advocating them as a cure, but as a small piece of a big puzzle. As one signpost on a challenging road; as one oar to help some paddle to the shore; as one small flicker of hope; as one way to diffuse the white.

For those of you struggling ... believe this. It is my deepest wish that somehow the words of this book can forge through the density of your white to open up a small yet tangible path to your yolk. Remember this: 'yolk' has the letter 'L' in it for Love ... but not the yoke. And if you can go within and find the love in your yolk it may lead you to that path.

The story of Kev

My brother had a very close friend called Kev. He was one of those men who was the true salt of the earth; grounded and humble, quiet, measured and modest. His yolk was full of all the attributes that make a man a true gentleman and humble hero. Kev was the type of friend you could always rely on. He was evergreen. He was a constant in all of our lives, often at our home when my brother and I were growing up. He was always there in the background, never making a fuss.

The irony is that when these quiet types are no longer in our lives, we notice their absence all the more intensely. It's as if the quietness of their demeanours leaves a greater noise in their absence. Kev was one of those people, and his sudden passing left an indelible hole in many people's lives.

None of Kev's closest friends were aware he was suffering with depression. He kept it hidden, and managed in silence until he could manage no more. He sadly took his own life.

On the day of his passing, Kev's brother went to my brother's house to inform him. He wanted my brother to be the one to tell Kev's closest mates. My brother called his friends to ask them to come over to his house. He then went outside and waited in the front courtyard for their arrival. My brother lives in inner-city Melbourne, where the gardens are small. A large currawong was sitting on the front fence. A bird of this size is an unusual sight in an inner-city courtyard.

The currawong was very close to my brother but did not move an inch. The bird looked directly at him with that connecting gaze I myself have experienced many times. It then flew away.

My brother knew without a shadow of a doubt that it was Kev who had orchestrated this meeting, this connection, this signal of his departure but also his ongoing presence. These occurrences are inexplicable, but leave no doubt in the mind of the observer that they are orchestrated by a departed loved one. It's the sense that the how and why are not known but paradoxically there is no doubt.

Many years later, Kev's favourite Australian Football League team, Richmond, won the Grand Final. After a long dry spell from winning a premiership, this indeed would have been a day Kev would have loved. My brother is a caricaturist and does work for the Australian Football League. He decided to honour his mate Kev by placing his initials on the drawing of the premiership cup. Just after finishing this drawing, my brother went in from his studio to the kitchen to have breakfast. While making a cup of tea, he was startled by a very loud cry of a bird. He opened the door and saw a large currawong sitting in the backyard.

Again, my brother and the bird looked at each other for what felt like minutes. The currawong had a slender grey beak, large head, white wing tips and soulful eyes. It looked directly at my brother, then flew away. This was the only time my brother had seen a currawong since the day Kev passed on.

My brother mentioned the currawong to another mutual friend of Kev's. He knew of the bird as it was apparently his favourite. That weekend this friend sent my brother a photo of his children while on holidays. A currawong sat on the balcony just three feet from the children. My friend had commented that Kev had come to pay them a visit.

Kev was one of the first spirits to come to me while meditating. He has said the currawong was his 'calling card', and he would come to my brother at his favourite camping site on the Murray River. My brother and his extended family visit this secluded and serene site every Easter. As promised, my brother was quietly sitting alone by the river bank enjoying the solitude when he looked up to find himself surrounded by currawongs.

It brings him great comfort knowing his friend is still watching.

Now some will say these events are coincidental, but for many of us – such as my brother and me – they are a clear and comforting sign from Kev, to show us connection never wavers, even after death.

I believe, in his later years, Kev struggled to find that trail through the thickened white, to reach his yolk. I think his depression made it increasingly difficult for him to tap in and find that inner light.

On that tragic day of Kev's death, he took his own shell. But his yolk lives on. When he appears to me in essence, his yolk is still the same Kev we all knew and loved; the gentle, humble, wise soul who is still with us, but just in spirit. He is still as invested in his family and friends, and the love he still feels for them is palpable.

These connections are like links in a chain that are solid and unbreakable.

Friendships formed live on; the love that is shared remains with us. Death can take our shells but it cannot touch our yolks. We can still have the meaningful connections we forged in our lifetimes. We all have the ability to draw strength and comfort from this if we choose.

Set Sail

Pay no attention
to this stale state of mind
Watch night falling, apathy enveloping time
Heavy heart, empty core, ambition astray
How did you ever get to feel this way?

What exactly are you waiting for?
What needs to be restored?
To project you to your destiny
Propel you so far forward

It's up to you, this is your time
Wait no, want no more
No paradigms, let spirits soar
One step, many steps, go forth

Be bold, be brave, embrace and own
Be all you are meant to be
Swim to your shore, face all head on
Set sail, set sail, be free

BERNADETTE SOMERS

Indecision may
wind your road
Fear may forge hills
and valleys
But the path to love
is straight
If your heart leads
the way

BERNADETTE SOMERS

YOLK PRACTICES

List 1: Love your yolk

To start the process of applying the steps in the book there are some exercises you can do as you venture through the yolk journey.

First, we need to learn how to tap in, how to discover what you love about your yolk, your essence, your qualities; what makes you unique and loveable.

TAP IN

While in your quiet time, your me time, your reflection time, write down a long list of what you *love about your yolk*.

No-one is going to read it but you, so do it freely and honestly. Write everything you can think of.

Sit for a while, and then write some more.

Take your time, and then read everything you have written.

Now imagine these qualities being spoken about in your eulogy.

List 2: What is my yolk asking me to love?

This is the harder list to write.

What parts of yourself do you reject, dislike, deny or ignore?

What is your yolk trying to get you to love? Does your yolk love your shell?

It is imperative for your yolk to love your shell as it works through it.

This list will help you to see whether you are truly loving yourself unconditionally. It will also help you to see what is holding you back.

How are you going to show these qualities to everyone?

How are you going to love these parts of you more?

How are you going to honour yourself, respect yourself, value yourself until you love every facet of you?

Write another list of what small step you can take today to love what your yolk is asking you to.

This will become your 'action list'. This is what you need to do to create change.

3. Understanding your shell

HOW HAVE WE become a society that defines people by the limitations and confines of their shells?

Our shells are our external and superficial layer, with which we present ourselves to the world. They are our exoskeletons, defined by our appearance, our gender and our age. But they are *not* a true representation of what we have within, our true essence, our unique blueprint and our core – our yolk.

Focusing on our shells disconnects us from our yolks, and prevents us from connecting on a deeper level with each other. They are the representation of us but may not truly represent what is beneath, what is within.

If our yolks are like our souls, our shells are like our bodies, the home for our yolks. The shells need to be accepted and loved for our yolks to thrive, as it's through the physical form of our shells that the yolks can be expressed.

The problem with society is we judge and discriminate against people by their shells, and we judge our own shells too. To live in alignment is to live with acceptance of our shells and their limitations, and to love our yolks.

APPEARANCE

We are all susceptible to judgements and stereotypes, whether it be of our appearance, our gender or our age. Stereotypes are often seen as a necessary mechanism to more quickly process information. Judging people by their appearance categorises them, but also limits them to the potentials of that stereotype. True potential is not housed in the shells of individuals, it is found within, in the yolks.

We all have different shells – different races, cultures, skin tone, hair colour, eye colour and appearance. We all look unique. But behind all our shells is a constant and unanimous want, and that is to feel a sense of belonging. It's part of the basic fabric of humanity, and it's what we all seek.

People spend so much money presenting their shells as the best versions of themselves, to improve their appearance and attractiveness, but spend very little on the practices that enhance their yolks. Our self-worth is often too entangled in the appearance of our shells and governed by the things that will ultimately wither in time. It's a no-win situation.

The younger generation use technology and social media to present their shells in the best possible light. Photos are modified,

UNDERSTANDING YOUR SHELL

cropped and air brushed, all in an attempt to present an inauthentic portrayal of normal. They seek validation and approval, chasing 'likes' on social media, without remembering the primary importance of self-love and approval.

I believe there is nothing wrong with self-love of the shells, so long as we love our yolks more. So long as we know that our shells will change with time, with the natural ebb and flow and inevitable cycles of life. If we accept and allow this to unfold with grace and ease, and not resist the inevitable process. If we learn to value what's within. We all have to make peace with our shells for our yolks to shine through them.

By redefining ourselves to prefer the inside more than the outside, to love more what's within, we could learn to connect more with our yolks and disconnect with our shells. We could be more accepting of our appearance and perceived flaws. We could be led comfortably through the natural cycles of life, honouring our yolks and caring less about the withering of our shells.

Our yolks have the ability to connect us all; they are the common thread that unites us. In seeing each others' yolks, we can find the common ground, we can understand each other and have empathy for one another. If we look beyond the shells and see the yolks, we see we are all inextricably connected and therefore we all belong. No-one is segregated or isolated.

After we have lived our lives, it's not the shells people remember, it is the qualities and uniqueness of the yolks. It is the kindnesses and courage, the love and the caring, the generosity and the giving. It is the yolks that are honoured, not the shells. So, to live life from this place of honouring what's within must be a step towards happiness.

But how often do we really try to get to know each others' yolks? How often do we judge people by their shells? How much time do we allow when meeting someone for the first time to connect with their yolks? Or have we already formed opinions and made assumptions based on their shells? Do we disconnect or decide they are not our 'type' based on their shells? Or do we have an open mind and open heart and look for the true expression of their yolks?

In our shell-fixated society we are all too quick to judge people by their shells, and these stereotypes and judgements can prevent the most meaningful connections from being birthed, preventing us from connecting on a deeper level. Connecting is the beginning of belonging, our very basic need and want.

The irony of this is that when we express our yolks and show our vulnerabilities, others *will* connect with us because deep down we all have fears and vulnerabilities – it's part of our human experience. We relate to others, have empathy for others, we like honesty and openness. If others express their yolks, it gives us permission and the opportunity to do the same. It opens the door for us to show our authentic selves, behind our shells. That process enables us to evolve and grow. Empathy becomes the byproduct of connection.

Judging others by their shells creates negative karma. It always results in us being judged ourselves and by ourselves. Acknowledging others' yolks creates positive karma.

Part of this process of judging others inadvertently means our shells become our armour, our thick skins, and our shields to hide our vulnerabilities. When everyone drops the armour, we are all exposed together and therefore all equal. Breaking out from behind our shells means we are set free from our old stories, our conditioning, our limits and our fears. We sit in the space that allows life to progress for us, to open up, for opportunity and experience to present.

GENDER

I believe gender stereotypes affect self-expression, expression of our yolks. I think how we choose to express ourselves, our thoughts, our actions, should not be governed by gender. Living a fully expressed life should feel free and liberating and should not feel defined or limited by gender. Living a life not fully expressed – for whatever reason – may lead to issues with emotional health.

I have three sons and one daughter, so I live in a household where the ratio is more males to females. I grew up in a large family with four brothers (and two sisters), and through my brothers' friendships and peer groups, have experienced the ripple effect of poor emotional health in men. Through depression, anxiety and even suicide. I care deeply about men's health, primarily men's emotional health and wellbeing.

Depression and anxiety are becoming more widespread in our community, and the incidence of suicide is higher in men than in women. Society often views men exposing their yolks – exposing their vulnerabilities – as 'unmanly'. Society has rules as to how men should act, and being vulnerable and emotional is generally seen as being weak.

I believe masculinity needs to be remodelled to make it acceptable to be emotional, to be vulnerable, to be authentic. Emotions are not just for girls; we are all born with them, and if they are bottled up we will not thrive.

I want my three sons to live by a new code of masculinity, and for my father and my brothers to embrace it too. I want my husband and sons to show vulnerability, and know that it is okay to do so. I want the term 'man up' to be replaced with the term 'open up', so that it's acceptable for all men to open up, drop the masculine armour and reveal their authentic selves.

I want society to acknowledge that crying is as acceptable for men as it is for women. That opening up and sharing feelings is courageous, not weak. That bottling up emotions and subscribing to the old 'stiff upper lip' mentality is no longer cool, nor acceptable.

I want couples to express their feelings to each other instead of the female doing so while the male shuts down. I want there to be many more networks and support groups specifically for men.

In our society we often tend to support a female who has experienced a miscarriage or stillborn baby, but often neglect the male. We often have stereotypes that it's the male's role to support the female at times of loss and grief, and go unsupported himself. We hear of many women's circles and women's networks which provide a framework for women to share and voice their feelings. But we don't appear to place as much value on men doing the same.

Look where that is getting us. In Australia in 2017, the Black Dog Institute found that 75% of suicides were males, and an estimated one-third of men are at risk of suffering from depression.

The more families I talk to, the more I have come to realise that the long, wretched arm of depression reaches many, leaving few families free from its grasp. These days we almost all know someone who suffers from depression or who has taken his or her own life. Homosexual men are even more at risk and more vulnerable, as they don't fit the outdated stereotype of how a man should act. Expressing emotions is still sometimes described as being 'gay'.

For men's mental health to improve, we all have to change our perspective, we all have to see that vulnerability is an asset for men, not a liability. That cracking open the shell of an outdated stereotype and revealing the yolk is the way forward. Regardless of gender, we are all hard-wired the same. Our shells define gender, not our yolks. Our yolks are genderless.

The LGBTQ community is a very vulnerable group in our society, and the blurred lines of gender and male stereotypes make it even harder for homosexual men to fit in. The only way forward is for us to ignore the shells, the variations, the categories, the superficialities.

The shells separate us all into categories: straight, gay, fat, thin, black, white, young, old. It's all irrelevant, it's all superficial – and it all creates separation. This can create great difficulties for the marginalised who cannot be 'boxed' into a category; transgender or interracial people, for example.

On 15 November 2017 in Australia the marriage equality vote was passed, with a 61% majority of the country supporting same-sex marriage. On that day I was very proud to be Australian. The outpouring of emotion, the relief, the happiness in the LGBTQ community was overwhelming. Television, websites, social media and talkback radio were inundated with emotional stories from gay people who had always felt non-acceptance from society. Through tears they described their darkest times, feeling they didn't belong, feeling judged by their shells.

Our shells define our sexual orientation but do not reveal our authenticity in our yolks. Whether we love men, women or both is irrelevant. Our true identity is in the yolk. The essence of who we are is not determined or lessened by our sexual orientation. It should not exclude anyone from equal rights. Our fundamental need is to belong, and with similar yolks, we all should. We should not base belonging on the identity of our shells.

The depth of emotion displayed on 15 November exemplifies how truly important it is to be loved and accepted and not swayed by the judgement of our shells. We all want love and we all want acceptance. We all want to belong. When we have this, we can thrive and evolve. When we don't, we stagnate. It's pivotal in our personal development and in our spiritual development. None of us want to live a life defined and dictated by the appearance of our shells.

AGE

We live in a world obsessed with anti-ageing, and in a society that seems to place so much value on youth and turning back the clock.

Our television screens, newspapers and social media are full of images of the young and air brushed, the wrinkle free and vital. Society stamps us all with a use-by date that is neither fair nor realistic. The obsession with youth seems to be worsening with each generation as the resistance to ageing gracefully intensifies. The quest for eternal youth now entraps men as well as women.

The older population are often undervalued in the workplace, and are often retrenched at age 50 as if their age is an expiry date. Age discrimination is a constant workplace threat, with those who are older viewed as having outdated skillsets and decreased performance. Seniors are often overlooked for new positions while their younger counterparts are seen as the safer and better choice. We are often seen as 'best before 50', and are viewed as less attractive, less employable and of less value past that age. With our older population growing in numbers, the risk of age stereotyping in the workplace will increase.

Our older generations have valuable wisdom to impart to the younger generations, with older workers bringing a wealth of experience and wisdom to the workforce. Sadly, these attributes are often overlooked or undervalued.

Age stereotypes whittle away self-worth. Judging others and judging our own withering shells has a significant impact on well-being and self-esteem. Ageing could be better embraced if we learnt to place less value on the shell and more value on the ageless yolk.

Inside when we connect with our yolks, we all feel the same, even though our shells display different numerical ages. We feel emotions, we love the same, and our hopes and dreams can be the same. We all still need to be loved, nurtured and accepted. We need our voices to be heard, and for our opinions to be acknowledged and valued.

To become a more tolerant and progressive society, we should think about ways in which we could place more value on the yolks of our aged population and be less discriminative towards their shells. It's imperative for us to love our shells regardless of their age, appearance or gender.

As an example of an ageless yolk, let me introduce the story of Ellen, a beautiful woman who never let age disguise her majestic yolk.

The story of Ellen

My Nana, Ellen, was a truly beautiful lady with a kind, devoted and loving yolk. She was incredibly wise, thoughtful, gentle and caring.

Ellen lost her husband, Robert, many years before her own passing. Robert, or Bob as he was known, was 10 years her senior and died 25 years before her. Because Nana was 10 years younger than Bob, she always felt younger than her peers. She seemed to possess that ageless quality, never really feeling her age or letting it define her. Even in her 90s she felt she was a little young for the residents in the aged care facility, despite most of them being younger than her. My family often found it amusing when Nana chose not to socialise with the residents as she found them too old.

I believe my Nana was one of those lucky and special people who didn't let her ageing shell define her worth. I would love to believe that, as a result, she lived to the extraordinary age of 100; that not feeling her age equated to living longer.

She passed 10 days after her 100th birthday, spending that day surrounded by her loving family, then quietly passing away late in the evening, half an hour after we had all left. It was as if she even had a say in the private and dignified way she made her exit.

Nana spent her last year essentially confined to her small room at the aged care facility, but was blessed to have many family members visit. As I'm part of a large family, she still had many who loved her and valued her. Her life was enriched by the connections of her immediate family, who looked beyond her shell to truly love her yolk.

When Nana was alive, I loved to talk to her about stories of the departed making their presence felt. I loved to hear her tell me how she still felt my grandfather, Bob, was still close, watching over. She often said she hoped Bob would still be waiting for her, despite so many years elapsing since his passing. I never doubted he would be waiting, and I think deep down she thought the same.

One night Nana had a vivid dream of her husband Bob lying next to her on his side of the bed. In the dream he was hugging her and reassuring her of his love and ongoing presence. The dream felt so real. When she woke, she was puzzled by a strong scent of leather in the room.

Bob had been a shoemaker, and this leathery scent was often his signature smell. When he was at work in the small workroom at the rear of their property, this particular scent filled the space and seeped into his clothes and skin. My grandmother knew the scent well.

To her disbelief, the bed covers on the other side of her bed had been pulled back, despite her sleeping on her side of the bed. Nana truly believed her loving Bob had paid her a visit during the night to reassure her that he was still ever present.

I now, in turn, often feel the loving presence of my grandmother. I can sense her wise words of encouragement and support. She used to call me her 'treasured possession' – a special name she had just for me. I now feel this book is one of my treasured possessions that honours her memory, honours her yolk.

And I truly believe my Nan gave me the strength to write it.

I have a camellia plant growing in my garden that was given to me by my mother in my grandmother's memory. My mother bought a camellia for all Nana's granddaughters and the grandson's wives.

I often find my camellia in bloom on particular days that I'm thinking of my Nan. I'm certain she watches over me with love. As the years elapse after her passing we all remember her and talk about the growth of our camellia plants. Some are in pots, some in the garden, some are growing well, and some not as well as others. I believe this is similar to our different lives and different paths: we are all doing the best we can given the soil, water and sunlight we are exposed to.

I still receive guidance from my Nana in spirit, and I am still so supported by her wise and loving advice. I dream of her often, just like she dreamed of her beloved Bob. Our deceased loved ones can often appear to us in our dreams, when our conscious or rational mind is sleeping. Often when we wake up, the dream can feel extremely vivid and real. I believe we should never discount the information conveyed to us in our dream state, and that we all have the potential to tap into this line of communication and connection.

I believe all our dreams can be sweet.

THE SHELL OF SOCIAL MEDIA

The message in this book is about *connection:* our brains are naturally wired to connect, and human connection is pivotal for our personal development and survival.

But what happens when this process of connection backfires? How do we address the issue of *over-connectivity* in our modern world? Our collective dependence on mobile devices, social networks and the internet is becoming a major issue.

Smartphones are now our telephone, diary, notepad, encyclopaedia, calendar, camera, photo album, alarm clock, torch and map – and that's just the beginning. Our lives and their sense of order are neatly packaged into the versatile capabilities of our phones. Is it any wonder our dependence on our devices is bordering on addiction?

Today's modern method of supposedly facilitating connection through social media is actually contributing to more people feeling disconnected, anxious and isolated through this passive means of communicating. Sites such as Facebook and Instagram not only quantify users' friendships – purportedly measuring their popularity – but broadcast the social functions and other fantastic activities that everybody else is doing, increasing feelings of exclusion and isolation. To make matters worse, people often scroll through social media in an effort to relieve their feelings of loneliness.

We have a problem.

This constant process of passive over-connectivity is rendering us all disconnected and further removed from active, authentic, human bonding. The art of connection involves paying genuine attention to each other: it involves the use of our senses to listen and make eye contact, and to use our intuition and touch. This cannot occur effectively through the shell of the internet.

Addictions are manifestations of numbing; numbing the pain, the boredom, the loneliness. They distract the mind from facing the truth. Addictions to social media contribute to this numbing. Switching off our phones forces us to be less distracted and pay more attention to ourselves, to the present moment.

Disconnecting from social media can assist us to reconnect with ourselves, with our yolks. It can allow us to be more anchored in our present state of circumstances and feelings rather than in a state of partial awareness. Social media only serves to take our attention away from ourselves, our yolks, and the more important aspects of our inner selves.

We have a duty of care to ourselves and to the younger generations to lessen the fallout of our over-connected and dependent society and find our way back inwards. We have to disengage from social media and re-engage with ourselves and others, yolk to yolk, not through the shell of social media.

4. Expressing your yolk

A LIFE WITHOUT FEAR

Once we have learnt to love our yolks and we have tried to live beyond the stereotypes and limitations of our shells, we must examine fear, which is the single biggest factor that prevents us from expressing our yolks. Fear is the number one enemy; it's our armour, and it's embedded into our shells. It prevents us from showing up, and from showing up for *ourselves*.

Imagine a life without fear.
We would …
… enrol in that course …
… apply for that job …
… learn that instrument …
… start that business …
… ask that person out on a date.

We would take chances and not be deterred by rejection, or even just the possibility of rejection. We would care less – or not at all – about judgement and being judged. We would in turn not judge others.

We would not be bound by the confines of our shells; we would dive head first into the unknown and the uncertain. We would take life boldly by the hands and embrace it, open up to it and truly live. We would make the most of our opportunities and make the most of our potential. We would live life freely in pursuit of what truly inspires us. We would have no need or desire to stay safe and small, avoiding risk.

Pushing through fear can allow true expression of our potential. Cutting through the fear in our shells makes us vulnerable, but it's one of the most courageous things we can do. It opens us up to more: more possibilities, more experiences, more learning and more growth. In the absence of fear we can reveal our true selves, our dreams, our hopes and our passions. In our raw and open states, we are vulnerable but more authentic.

A truly expressed yolk enables us to live a fully expressed life. Expression involves exposure and courage.

Expressing our yolks means tapping into what inspires us, what drives us, what aligns us. Inspiration drives our creative instincts to be expressed. When we are living in alignment with our expressed yolks, we feel connected and present. We feel we are contributing and making a difference; a difference to our own lives and the lives of others.

We all have something we feel we are called to do; to help, to heal, to care, to inspire, to create, to engage, to teach. When we tap into our yolks to discover this potential, life presents us with opportunities for expression.

EXPRESSING YOUR YOLK

First, we love ourselves and discover what is innate in us. Then, we show up; one day, one step at a time. We ask what needs to be done to express our yolks, what needs to be birthed. We show up, we say we are ready to brave vulnerability, and we take action.

Life is meant to sit us in the sweet spot between comfort and discomfort in order to stretch and grow. Expressing our yolks equates to stretching; tapping into our unique blueprint and taking action. Action just means showing up and committing to taking a step forward; it doesn't mean knowing the whole plan. It just means following the thread. It means showing up and saying how can we teach today, how can we create today, how can we write today? It's about being prepared to try, to have a go, to be ready, eager and enthusiastic. It means looking fear in the eye and venturing forward regardless.

Once we show up, the ducks can line up, as life is just waiting for us to tap into our potential. But it can't happen unless we take some form of action. We are the key to the lock that opens the door of potential. The door *wants* to open. Life waits for us and wants to usher us through the door, but we have to take the first step.

I believe that's how we find purpose, how we find our path. We just need to tap into the potential, the talents, the possibilities of our yolks and be ready to express them. We just need to connect within and express what's within, then allow life to steer us in the direction we are meant to go. It shouldn't be complicated, we just need to trust and follow the thread.

We need to trust that the qualities of our yolks are *meant* to be expressed. We are meant to have a fully expressed life; that is the point of it all. If we feel off track, we are not expressing our yolks, not showing up, or not taking action, or all three.

Life provides many opportunities, many synchronicities, many chances for us to be guided. Opportunities that appear out of the blue, possibilities that present out of nowhere; these are our signs. Love must come first; we must love our innate qualities to inspire, create, teach, help, engage, nurture. Love who we are, discover what we love, and then we can express it.

Expression is all about connection. We are all here to express our yolks in order to serve others. There is no point writing if no-one will read, there is no point healing if there is no-one to heal, there is no point teaching if there is no-one to teach.

Expression is for connection. That is the point. It's all for the greater good. It's all about serving others. Tapping into our yolks and expressing our potential enables us to serve others. We are *supposed* to live a life of connection; connection to ourselves and connection with others.

To live a life of connection equates to living a fully expressed life. To live a fully expressed life means that we are connected.

Life is about being present, being in the here and now, and really absorbing every moment. If we take the time to smell the roses, we discover that we are the actual scent. Life is not meant to be a race, and it's not meant to be a struggle. Yet too many of us are standing on the weight we are trying to lift.

When we are quiet we can hear the guidance, we can notice the synchronicities, as life is always trying to work in our favour, to give us opportunities to realise our potential. We need to tap in, show up and be ready to express what's within. We need to really look at our innate qualities and talents, our skills and our callings, and then take the action required to express them. This expression may be revealed in a hobby, career, creative pursuit or passion. There are many ways to express our uniqueness and make the most of our skillsets.

Often people confuse their career choice with their calling. We *can* have happiness in our careers – but only if they are enabling us to express the innate qualities of our yolks.

Many people are stuck in careers that don't bring them happiness because their careers are not allowing the expression of their full potential. They have perhaps chosen a career that is not aligned with their innate talents, or they are not feeling the connection that comes from expression.

They are not expressing their yolks.

We all have a choice to align our happiness with the thing we are spending most of our lives doing. We have options – life is not fixed. We can look for ways to combine happiness with our career. We can follow our passions and still make an income from the pursuit.

Feeling trapped in a career that doesn't bring happiness comes from a mindset of being stuck. It's also entangled with fear, often fear of loss of income. We need to realise that fear is the obstacle to overcome in order to be happy. We need fear to make us stretch, to strive, to dust ourselves off and learn resilience; we need challenges and obstacles to grow. If we break through our shells of fear, we can have great achievements and personal triumphs. We can take the chance to show the true grit, strength, and character of our yolks.

Too many of us are racing to the finish line and we have lost sight of what we are racing for. In all the rush, in all the busyness of our lives, we have little time for reflection. When we make time for reflection we can get in touch with our own yolks. When we reflect, we can really analyse where we are heading with our lives, our direction, our choices and our happiness.

Often it's in those seconds before we fall asleep that we might find a moment to reflect. But most of us use that time to rewind the day's events and focus on the past rather than the present. Alternatively, we use that quiet time to schedule tomorrow's events and entangle our thoughts in the future.

It's like we spend our whole lives searching for a hidden treasure when all the time it is in fact buried deep within. When we find the time for reflection, we can work out what qualities of our yolks need to be expressed; we can access that buried treasure. We all have an opportunity in this one shot at life to be doing something that brings us happiness. We all have the right to enjoy what we do, and are not meant to be bored, uninspired or entangled.

To express our yolks, our unique blueprint, we have to ask ourselves the hard questions. We need to work out what potential is not being utilised, what talents and skills are not being used and expressed. We need to look deep within and ask ourselves what is holding us back. Is it fear? Or risk of judgement? Is it lack of motivation? Or apathy? Is it lack of confidence or self-belief?

Asking these questions can often show us we still haven't mastered self-love. We haven't yet learnt to love ourselves unconditionally. Because when we fully love ourselves, we have confidence, we don't worry about judgement, we are motivated and inspired to be the best versions of ourselves.

Often, all the reasons hindering our ability to express our yolks stem from lack of self-love. Take a moment to let that sink in, and think about the first step of this code: love your yolk. Realise, right here and now, that when you achieve this, everything changes. You cannot live a fully expressed life unless you have self-love.

Know that our starting point must be a mindset of being happy and loving for the doors of opportunity to open up. Know that energy works in favour of happiness attracting happiness, like attracting like. Remember there are forces working every day in every way to guide us towards achieving our potential and making the most of all our gifts.

The answers are in our yolks, the deepest parts of us, the absolute best expressions of us, and they are calling us where we all know we need to go. Happiness awaits us there.

Leap of Faith

Wash away the stains
Air dry the thoughts
Cleanse and surrender
Unfathomable, the feeling
Clarity

It's all for nothing, all in vain
If not for the now
This moment, this space in time
This is all, this is now

Why wait, procrastinate
Take your leap of faith
Trust the process.
All awaits you.
Just leap …

BERNADETTE SOMERS

Now let's look at two major influences in our lives that can potentially help us encourage and express our unique blueprints in our yolks: our parents and our education.

THE PARENT YOLK

Parenting is a role we can play without any qualifications, experience or training. The position comes without a manual or guidebook, and many of us have no option other than to trial-and-error our way through.

Many of us stumble through the parenting years, drawing on instinct and our own experiences of being parented, whether by our biological, adoptive or foster parents. We all run the risk of repeating the same patterns of parenting, be those patterns favourable or unfavourable. We all take on habits, styles and conditionings from our parents, and we may try to emulate our parents if the experience was deemed positive. Alternatively, we may strive to parent very differently if our experience was less than optimal. Unfortunately, our children are our 'test runs', and the cycle is reproduced when they in turn reach parenthood. Our choices of parental styles drastically affect the development of our children and potentially are replicated by them.

We are linked by the collective quest to try to do our best despite the hurdles, and we are in the role until we take our last breath, whether we like it or not. Sadly, many are ill equipped. Some are too young, too old, too stressed, too invested, too uninterested, too tired, too self-absorbed, or too time poor to do the job well.

My own personal belief is that our role as parents needs to be redefined. We need to view the task of parenting with a new perspective. I believe our primary role as parents is one of custodians.

We are required to provide the essential and foundational needs of food, shelter, and a big dose of love. The main provision is of course love. It is the most basic requirement for children to thrive.

Our children are not our possessions, and are not in our possession. They are individuals on their individual journeys, playing their own individual board games of life. It is therefore not our job to control this path or direct our children where we believe they should go. It is their path and their life.

Our primary aim should be to provide them with a safe, loving and secure environment to encourage their yolks, their unique expression. Although they are from us, they are not meant to live their lives following our paths – they must choose their own.

We need to teach our children to express their yolks. Show them their yolks so we can show them the way. Our role is to help them find themselves; their talents, their qualities, their passions and their creative skills. We must love their yolks and encourage them to love their own.

We can teach them not to hide within their shells but embrace their uniqueness and utilise their potential. We can help them to cultivate their yolks by putting practices in place to keep them balanced; plenty of time outdoors in nature, healthy friendships, fresh air, good food and lots of love and support.

Our children are like seeds planted in the earth. We have little say and little control over what will bloom. But we need to provide the right conditions, water and sunlight for them to grow. What blooms from this is their call, their birthright, not ours. It may not resemble our blooms. Our job is to tend to our own blooming, cultivate our own garden.

Parenting is like a delicate dance of staying close and keeping a gentle distance. Encouraging and releasing. Championing and retreating. We must try to honour our children's rights to direct their own paths, play their own board games, bloom their own flowers. We can do this gentle dance with love. We should do this with love, as love is the foundation, love is the soil. We must encourage their yolks as much as we must encourage our own.

Often our job as parents feels layered with guilt and pressure. Are we doing enough, or too much? And are we doing things right ... whatever that means? Maternal and paternal instincts make us want to protect our children at all costs, and protecting them can often lead to controlling them. We feel better equipped to protect them if we have more say, more control over the board game. But sometimes we have to surrender control. Sometimes we need to anchor our children to our support and love while giving them enough freedom to explore their own path.

Our role is to encourage them to play their own board game. It is *their* game, not ours. We play our own game, we walk our own road. We can nurture and support them, guide and encourage them, but we can't control them.

I believe if we start early and teach our children to discover their yolks, connect within and express their potential, we can take the passenger seat and allow our children to sit in the driver's seat.

The story of Cathy

I met my friend Cathy through the local primary school. Our children were of similar ages, and our daughters attended dance class together.

Cathy's yolk was beautiful, devoted, kind and loving. She was deeply committed to her family and close friends. She was honest, open, light hearted and friendly. She was expecting her fourth child, a girl, already named Sophie.

Cathy epitomised the type of parent who was fully invested in her children. She was a loving and caring mother who encouraged the yolks of her children, guiding them without orchestrating their paths.

Cathy was nearing the end of her pregnancy and was home nesting and preparing for the impending arrival of baby Sophie. It was mid-January and school holiday time, that relaxed time to rest up and prepare for a new school year and a new baby. Cathy's husband was at work, and by chance she was home alone.

Without warning Cathy felt incredibly unwell, and urgently rang her husband at work. He called an ambulance and left work immediately. By the time he arrived home he found her gravely ill. The ambulance arrived soon after and Cathy was taken to the closest hospital, with her husband following in his car.

As he was following, the ambulance siren was switched off and the rapid pace of the vehicle lessened. He knew instantly that things were not good. He arrived at the hospital to learn that Cathy had passed away, as had her unborn baby girl.

Our friend's life had been irrevocably changed on this tragic day. He lost his beautiful wife and unborn baby, and was left to raise three young children on his own. The whole school community and neighbourhood was so heartbroken for him and his three children. It seemed so tragic and unfair.

Our friend moved forward with his life and did his best to raise his children with the help of a young nanny he employed to assist him. After a few months he decided he needed to get away from everything, and he decided to take a road trip to Queensland with his children and the nanny.

They all needed a change of scenery and to escape the sadness at home. Along the journey he developed feelings for the nanny, and she did for him too. On arriving in Queensland, they found love in each other's arms.

The next morning our friend awoke and wandered onto the balcony.

He was thinking about Cathy and about the new hope that had brought love back into his life. As he stood on the balcony, two rainbow lorikeets flew in very close to where he was standing. They looked straight at him and then began to lock beaks and kiss, as these birds are known to do.

They were within arm's reach of where he stood. Instantly he knew this was a sign from Cathy. This was her blessing to move forward with his life and embrace love again. It was her clear message to him.

The husband rang me from his holiday later that day and recounted that moment. We were both astounded and equally comforted by the events that were Cathy's message to him to move forward. I was so happy for him that he had found love again. I finished chatting to him and then went out to my kitchen and was thinking about the beautiful synchronicity that had occurred.

My middle son, who was five years old, came into the kitchen and asked me, 'What is the name of the bird with a blue head, green wings and red beak?' My son was fascinated with birds as his prep teacher had a canary named Sapphire which she kept in his classroom. 'I'm not sure,' I responded, not really thinking much about his question.

Later that day I was thinking about my son's question and decided to text my friend to ask him the description of the rainbow lorikeets he had seen. My son's description had been so specific. My friend told me that the birds had blue heads, green wings and red beaks. As fate would have it, these features are the hallmark of the rainbow lorikeet, the birds that appeared to my friend and were described by my son.

I don't believe any of this was a coincidence. I believe wholeheartedly that the lorikeets were used as messengers by Cathy to illustrate that her yolk lived on; that she was still watching over her husband and her children. Cathy was still supporting and encouraging them, still connecting to her family from the other side.

Our friend went on to marry his new love and have three more children.

I have no doubt that Cathy still watches over them all from above, loving her three children still living and her baby Sophie in spirit.

I find myself constantly in awe of these wonderful synchronicities which remind me of the wonder of life and after life. Whenever I start to second guess myself another wondrous occurrence unfolds again and again to lift my spirits and fill me with hope and comfort.

EXPRESSING YOUR YOLK

My hope is that you too find hope and solace in these stories. My hope is that you too are gifted with signs and messages from your loved ones as well. My hope is you will be touched by this magic and wonder as I am.

THE SCHOOL OF YOLK

I believe all parents want their children to be educated and encouraged, and to be taught how to best express the qualities of their yolks. Parents also want this education to occur in a safe, nurturing environment where their children feel a sense of belonging.

Children are more likely to thrive at schools which foster that basic need of belonging. That despite the academic results the students achieve, they are still part of the fabric of the school. It's paramount for schools to foster and cultivate belonging, so all students feel an integral part of the school, and feel a strong sense of camaraderie and connection. Research also suggests learning is enhanced when students feel secure and connected.

Having four children, I have journeyed through a number of different schools, both primary and secondary. I have sent my children to the local primary school and had the good fortune to send them to private secondary school. I've had numerous discussions with friends and family about different styles of education and finding the right fit for their children.

Children learn social behaviour by observation, and a lot of this observation takes place at school. They learn to identify different stereotypes, and some children can be harsh in judging other children by their shells. If students look, act or speak differently, they may be ostracised.

All of us, whether we are children or adults, have a fundamental need to belong, to feel accepted as part of a group. It is integral to us, in order to thrive and flourish as individuals. This is because of the basic underlying need and want to connect. Connection of our yolks is a basic and incredibly important need for us all. Often this is weighted as more important than academic potential by parents who value the overall emotional health and wellbeing of their children. Students who feel connected socially and feel a sense of belonging and acceptance are more likely to express their unique potential.

In the private school sector, I feel parents can become caught up in the cycle of performance and measurement. The schools need enrolments and the funds they provide. So, they push the academic achievements of their students so parents will enrol their children. The parents who pay good money to send their children to the school want value for their dollar.

The teachers' jobs are also under pressure – they need to produce good scores from their students to secure their positions. They need to produce the goods to reflect the merits of the school, to keep enrolments flowing and to continue the cycle.

In the middle of all this, the wellbeing of the students may not be the top priority.

This is business, right? This is how the school makes a profit. Well, I believe the education of our children should not be about business. The problem is the students are judged, measured and rated purely on their academic scores. They are judged by their shells. Not by their yolks.

The students might have empathy, gratitude, compassion, and deep core values. They might have highly creative minds and individualised ways of thinking. But their positive character traits may not factor into their ultimate results, their school achievements, their school successes. Their academic scores are based solely on their shells; numbers and scores. What lies within is of little relevance on this score sheet.

Students are generally taught to study to pass tests rather than equip themselves with knowledge to utilise for future benefit. They are often not taught to expand their minds and think outside of the 'academic box'.

Learning is often structured to be assessed by scores. It can often be uninspiring and is definitely not individualised to best suit each student.

The current system in Australia has many flaws. It places too much emphasis on academic achievement, the shell, the facade. Not enough emphasis is placed on cultivating the yolks of the students, nurturing individual talents and exploring all potential. There are alternative models of education which challenge old educational structures currently in place in countries such as Finland. They strive to develop the pupils' intellectual, artistic and practical skills in an integrated and wholistic manner.

Schools need to develop and nurture all talents, all potentials, not just the skillsets that match the rigid archetypes of the school's academic model. Our children should be taught the skills of innovation and exploration and to fearlessly pursue their passions and talents.

If the yolks were valued more than the shells, there would be class structures to assist children to connect with their yolks, to explore their passions, build their self-esteem, reveal their creative skills and build their confidence.

Teaching methods could alter to encourage more self-guided and individualised learning to facilitate students to identify their passions. Assessment could be modified to boost students' self-esteem instead of diminishing it with scores and rankings.

The current system of measuring every student by academic scores can often lead to diminished self-worth in vulnerable students. A system that rates and measures is bound to put pressure on the students already struggling with low self-esteem. We must ask, why do we need the scores? Is it to squeeze the very last drop of academic achievement out of our children to promote the school?

With the alarming increase of depression and anxiety in school-aged children, we have to carefully examine the current system and ask if it is right for every student. The pressure of achieving academic success is not the right fit for all students, as it may foster a motivation to cram for an exam but not equip them with life skills and life knowledge.

I believe many parents know the school system is not perfect but don't know where to begin to help fix the problem. They often just bide their time until their children are through. There are not a lot of alternatives available apart from home schooling, and the majority are too time poor and stretched to entertain that prospect.

How can we implement change?

I know it's simple, but couldn't the education system be less about scores and marks and more about cultivating self-esteem and self-worth? Do the scores really matter? Do they really serve our children? Aren't we all here to learn, evolve and grow, follow our passions and extend our talents and skills? Can't we do that in an environment that's not so competitive? Can't we inspire our children without forcing them into the same old education cycle without ever questioning its merit?

I wish for students to be inspired to learn, not cornered into just achieving scores. I care about their endeavour, and want them to learn – not cram. I want them to be in an environment in which they thrive, not just conform.

I wish I could enrol every pupil in my 'School of Yolk', where they have full say in the subjects they study and enjoy, rather than adhering to the same old core subject list. Where their learning is individualised and self-directed, abolishing exam scores and reports.

Pupils could choose the times best suited for optimal learning, and be exposed to an array of learning styles with the ability to explore creative pursuits. Education could be free and accessible to all students, abolishing the need for public and private sectors. All students could be taught to use their intellects to determine what they have an interest in learning. Pupils could learn how to express their yolks to learn how to live fully expressed lives.

As a wonderful representation of my School of Yolk, let me introduce the story of Margot, a teacher in her lifetime who tried to reflect those values.

The story of Margot

Margot was the beautiful mother of my sister in law. She was a smart, wise, caring and devoted woman who worked most of her life as a primary school teacher.

Margot's yolk was kind and fair, loving and warm, wise and thoughtful. She was the type of lady who seemed to have her finger on the pulse and knew what was required in any situation. She had that special quality that enabled her to teach, to impart her knowledge and foster the development of the children she came in contact with.

Margot taught for many years at the local primary school, and was well known and loved by many families. The community commemorated her by having a street near the school named after her.

I believe Margot was blessed with a career that enabled her to best express the innate qualities of her yolk. She was best suited to teaching and imparting her wisdom. It suited her soul and brought her immense joy. She spent her life doing what she did best, expressing the unique qualities of her yolk for the greater good of all the students who crossed her path.

Margot showed up every day to utilise her skills to better the lives of all that she taught. Margot was the type of teacher who always tried to encourage the yolks of her young students; she tried to look beyond their shells and really connect. She represented the kind of teacher best suited to teach at the 'School of Yolk'. She also utilised these skills as a parent, and taught her three children how to express the unique potential of their yolks.

Margot's daughter was a Physiotherapist and worked at the same hospital as me. It was through our friendship that my brother met his future wife.

Margot was diagnosed with an aggressive form of bowel cancer, and battled the disease for three months with a quiet resolve, strength and dignity. As she was approaching the end of her battle, she was often in my thoughts.

I was thinking about Margot one particular morning as I sat eating breakfast at the bench in my kitchen. The bench faced out into my garden, and was always a lovely place to sit and enjoy the view. This particular morning was very peaceful.

As I sat there absorbed in my thoughts about Margot, out of nowhere a beautiful bird swooped down from the sky and straight towards the window. It flew as close to the window as it could and looked me straight in the eye. It then swiftly flew away. It was of no irony that this bird swept in like Margot's cancer took her, abrupt and final. I knew instantly without a doubt that Margot had just passed away. This bird looked at me and through me as if it was delivering the message to me. Immediately after, my phone rang and it was my brother telling me that Margot had indeed passed.

This bird was a clear sign Margot was no longer in physical form and was passing over. I now no longer believe in coincidences; I believe in synchronicities. I believe we just cannot fully comprehend the order of all things. I believe we are trying to reconcile with the truth that all of us are interlinked into one big process; everything interrelates and fits into form.

The intricacy of it all is miraculous and exquisite. How it all unfolds is a mystery. Call it destiny, call it fate, call it magic, call

EXPRESSING YOUR YOLK

it truth; whatever is at play exists and is existing this very instant, even as you read this.

You might remember your own synchronicity or have your own realisations. Hopefully they are enabling you to see that you too are part of this big process.

When you tune in, it becomes so apparent. Evidence is everywhere. It's like we only have to find the right channel to tune in to. It's so simple, yet so powerful. It has the power to open us up and lift our spirits.

Margot's story reminds me of the absolute majesty of life; her teachings still live on in the hearts and minds of all her students. There is a permanence that death cannot shake. Margot lived her life expressing her yolk, helping, teaching and caring for her young students. That remains her legacy; that is her story.

YOLK PRACTICES

List 1: Express your yolk

Show up.

To help you to identify what qualities in your yolk need to be expressed, I recommend you do this exercise. Make a list of all the ways you are showing up and expressing your talents, passions, interests and skills. Write down all the ways you are successfully expressing your yolk.

List 2: What potential is your yolk calling you to express?

What would you do in your life and with your life if you had no fear?

What hidden talents have you that have never been expressed?

What is holding you back? What stereotype of age, gender, race, or appearance is limiting your expression?

Read your list and read it again. This is the list that holds the key to what you need to address.

This is where you are stuck. This is where you need to heal.

Start to formulate your *action* list of how you can make this happen.

What small step can you take *today* to begin to utilise the potential that your yolk wants you to?

Remember, we cannot let fear stand in our way. Fear is part of the shell and needs to be broken through to reach your yolk.

Remember, these qualities in your yolk are meant to be *utilised*. They are with you and in you for a reason. The yolk needs to work through those limitations of the shell to express itself; that is the challenge, that is the point, that is the growth.

Get thinking, get creative, make things happen and fill your thoughts with positivity and enthusiasm.

Spend a few minutes each day visualising that you have achieved this.

5. Cultivating your yolk

ONCE WE LEARN to love and express our yolks, we should try to learn the ways in which to cultivate them.

We need to try to embrace the practices that assist us in getting in touch with who we are and why we are here. From there we can continue implementing these practices to keep us aligned in that space.

There are many different ways to keep ourselves feeling aligned and balanced. There are ways we can remove ourselves from the hustle and bustle of life and bring ourselves back into balance. We might find that once we begin on this yolk journey, we might need to carve out a little time in each day to make these cultivating practices become an integral part of our day.

We might discover that we crave them; we need to find time in nature, we want to rid ourselves of toxic relationships, we need to simplify our lives and address our health. We may feel pulled to give back to our community, or want to learn how to meditate. We might find ourselves wanting to be by the sea, or by the mountains, or out in nature. We might feel inspired to take up a creative pursuit. We may even start to question the bigger picture of life and be drawn to more spiritual concepts or practices.

All of these callings are examples of being on a quest to find a little more meaning to life. They are the rumblings of inner change, a subtle and gentle unravelling of the old to usher in the new. They are the callings of finding a new way, a new path, a shedding of the old layers to reveal the fresh layers underneath.

These are all the changes and yearnings that happened to me as I began to unfold and change. As I learnt to love and express my yolk, I felt it was calling me to carve out some time to cultivate it. These practices became non-negotiable in my daily routine, to stay balanced and grounded. And it was from this place and space of connection to myself that the doorway opened up to connect with spirit.

Everything changed for me in a reasonably short period of time. I opened up to guidance and support, my intuition heightened, I understood the bigger picture at play in many of my life's scenarios, and I began to heal. I then began to receive guidance from spirit and my mediumship skills unfolded.

I followed the code: I loved my yolk, I began expressing myself, and I made time to incorporate the following seven areas of cultivation in my life.

If you are wanting to open up to more guidance and to feel the same connection as I do, you have the tools in this book to assist you. If you feel you are on some sort of quest to find more meaning in your life and believe there is guidance waiting for you to tap into but are not sure exactly how to, this is your book, this is your code.

The seven areas that need addressing to cultivate your yolk are:

- mindfulness
- nature
- creativity
- giving
- relationships
- health
- spirituality.

Let's have a look at each of these.

MINDFULNESS

One of the best ways to cultivate our yolks is through mindfulness. It's not only a practice that allows direct access to the yolk but it also *enhances* the yolk.

Mindfulness is the process of being present in order to have greater awareness of our thoughts, feelings, bodies and environment. Mindfulness and meditation are terms used to essentially describe very similar things. I like to differentiate the two by seeing mindfulness as the awareness and meditation as a way of practising this awareness. The two go hand in hand.

Mindfulness teaches us how to anchor in the present moment so we can shift our focus from *doing*. In this space we can just *be* – be present, be aware, and connect within.

I remember a time many years ago when I had three children under three. I was always tired and busy, and went through each day just focused on getting to the end of the day with all my tasks done. I then spent the small amount of 'me time' each evening thinking about tomorrow's to-do list. I bathed and changed my children, cleaned and fed them, did the laundry, played with them, attended the mothers' groups, the play groups, and whatever other groups seemed necessary. I kept it all together. I ran a tight ship. I was efficient and organised.

But today I do not have sharp memories of that time in my life. I wasn't really absorbing it all, savouring the time with my beautiful babies. I wasn't really present.

Around that time, I was asked to go to a psychic flower reading with two close friends, who were also mums. It was a bit of a novel and interesting thing to do. I needed to take one flower from my garden, put it in a paper bag and bring it to the group reading. The psychic would choose a flower and have a message for the anonymous owner.

I found the only flower in bloom in my garden; an azalea, growing surprisingly well in a limestone pot at the front door. I think this azalea thrived on neglect and an occasional water when I remembered it. It was a beautiful pink and mauve colour, and looked perfect. So off I went with flower in bag and pram and babies in tow.

The psychic stood at the front of a large room slowly working her way through the bags with flowers hidden inside. Slowly she got to my flower. She took it and examined it closely. Then she said the owner of this perfect flower needed to slow down, stop rushing, and make meditation a daily practice.

I remember feeling mildly annoyed. *Meditate*, I thought. *Who has the time to do that?* I was an incredibly busy young mother just keeping her head above water.

Looking back, I now know this was to be a very important message for me. It, however, took me years before I put that advice into action.

For me, personally, meditation was and still is a game changer. It's the best practice to instil mindfulness, gain perspective, reflect and find clarity.

It has changed me irrevocably for the better. It has grounded me. It has opened me up to a greater wisdom and guidance. It has enabled me to take stock and move forward with more presence and purpose. But the most important thing is my meditation practice has opened my doorway to connection. It is through meditation that I have connected within in order to better connect with others.

So much has swept past me in the river of my life, floating past like driftwood. So many moments were fleeting and not processed and treasured as they should have been. The busyness of life has often got in the way of me building wonderful memories to take with me as I journey forward. I unfortunately cannot press rewind.

A lot of my treasured memories of my children when they were young are hazy. I was going through the motions to get through my busy day. I was always behind the lens of my video camera trying to capture the moments to save as my memories. Maybe if I had put the camera down and been more present, I might remember everything with more clarity. Maybe all I needed was to just 'be' more in the moment, instead of trying to 'do' more.

I know I am not alone; there are so many time-poor, tired young mothers who feel just as I did, that the really precious moments could be better remembered and cherished if we weren't so busy and caught up in the next moment. If we just let go and relaxed and settled into the space of 'now', we could let go of the *doing* and focus more on *being*.

Mindfulness is one of the best practices to facilitate *being* not *doing*. It is the anchor to bring us back to the present. It enables us to break free from the constant entanglement with what's next. The next minute, hour, day or year is not reality. Only what's happening right now is real. What we pre-empt for the future is just an assumption, an idea. We waste so much time stressing about what might not even transpire. We entangle our minds in thoughts of the future. We chase the finish line without ever making progress.

We continually make our to-do lists but never contemplate our 'to-be' list because it is such a short list. All that is on our 'to-be' list is essentially to be happy. We can't 'do' happiness. We can only be it.

A lot of people are resistant to letting go of the *doing* to settle into the *being*. They can be a little unsettled just being still. They can be a little scared of what rises to the surface. They can use 'doing', the rushing, the turbulence, the action as a way of masking the truth.

When they quieten the mind to focus inward, they can be faced with the uncomfortable reality that all the 'doing' is not getting them any closer to where they want to be. When we go inward in the practice of meditation, we anchor, we gain a sense of self. It's there that we can find self-love.

Meditation is about focusing on our yolks. It's about going within, finding solace, reflection and quiet. In that space, in that stillness, we can connect with our yolks and let worries and fears fall away. In that space we may realise that all we have to do is live, bringing our yolks to the forefront, exposing them proudly and loving them dearly.

Mindfulness and meditation help us tune into the frequency of our own intuition, our own inner guidance system. Intuition is our direct link to our yolks. Our intuition, our 'gut feeling', is our body's way of communicating with us. It's our sixth sense. Too many of us don't hear the whisper of the intuition amid all the hustle of life. All the doing, all the rushing creates turbulence and noise, which drowns out the voice from within. Often when we continue to live in that state of turbulence, our bodies have no other option than to get our attention through ailment, something that makes us stop and listen. Something that forces us to pay attention.

Our intuition is always guiding us in the right direction and on the right path. We must take heed of the message and believe in the wisdom being offered to us. When we trust our intuition, it steers us on the path of least resistance and of alignment. It enables us to step in sync with our natural flow and follow the path we are meant to travel. We subtly know when we are off the path; things seem forced, controlled, obstacles are in our way, the road does not feel aligned.

We have to go inward, connect with our yolks and receive that guidance. We need to make a daily practice of quietening our minds to hear our intuition. We need to value more our inner guidance system so we stay on course.

Meditation is the best way to facilitate this, to enable us to hear what we need to hear, to be led without leading, to be guided by what feels right inside.

To trust in the process.

Intuition is the guidance from greater forces working in our favour. It's the tool to reach within to become more connected to everything and everyone. If you want more guidance and connection, mindfulness and meditation should be your first options.

If you are new to meditation, let me help you; let me provide the tools for your tool belt. Let us start off slowly together and begin to use these tools to help cultivate your yolk. You can go to my website Bernadettesomers.com to access your free Yolk Meditation. Trial it and see where it leads you. You don't have to know where you'll end up, you just have to take the first step.

One step is all I took, all those years ago; and now I find myself writing this book. See where the path leads you – if you allow it.

Now let's look at other ways to cultivate that beautiful yolk.

NATURE

Being outdoors, out in nature, cultivates our yolks. The reality is that not only does it connect us to our yolks, but to every living thing, every plant, every animal, every person.

Nature has the capacity to ground us. It calms and centres us, and allows us to sense the bigger picture at play. It can give us great clarity, and it can open the doors to inspiration.

Often my writing ideas and themes emerge from the space around me when I'm out walking in nature. I can sit at a computer and have writer's block, but I go out in nature and have creative ideas flow to me.

What is this magic, and how can we have more of this in our lives? How good does it feel to walk barefoot on fresh grass and feel it between our toes? How wonderful is it to swim in the ocean or walk on a sandy beach?

If you are finding you are drawn to spending time in nature, that you have to make time to unwind by the sea or reboot with a walk outdoors, you are already in tune with the whispers of your yolk. It's already intuitively guiding you on how to get back in balance. It's showing you how to cultivate it. Being in nature helps us to stop the rushing and find centre. I think it's in this very space that we become open to the field of opportunity and potential around us. It's as if being out in fresh air opens the window to our yolks, for inspiration and ideas to reach our creative centre.

Ask yourself whether you are creatively inspired after walking outdoors, or swimming in the ocean, or hiking up a mountain. Do you feel more aligned and energised? Do you have new ideas and creative thoughts after? Again, it is guidance that your yolk is being cultivated.

'Earthing' is a practice that has been around for many years. Walking barefoot on grass, sand or dirt puts our feet in direct contact with the earth, and the earth's energy harmonises and stabilises us. Our connection to nature and our planet is vital, and good for our general health and wellbeing. In helping us to find centre we can check in and tend to the needs we have deep within. It helps us to press the reboot button.

The same thread that draws us all to connect within is the same thread that connects us to each other. It's the thread of oneness, the common thread of humanity. It tugs at the hearts of us all, young and old.

Travelling the world and seeing all its beautiful sights and wonders is a conduit to provide this connection. Travel and its experiences are good for the soul. There is a quote that says, 'we travel not to escape life but that life does not escape us'. It opens our eyes to the world, and all its people we are connected to by this common thread.

Travel expresses nature to us, in all its different locations and treasures. How many of our young adults leave the nest to travel the globe and find themselves? It's like a rite of passage to adulthood. It challenges us to leave the safety net of home to broaden our horizons and cultivate our yolks. Travel is in essence the exploration of nature, and we all need the grounding nature provides. It enriches us. It cultivates our yolks.

If you are feeling drawn to travel and to different places and experiences, it may be your guidance to stretch your boundaries and mix things up a little. It might be your guidance system wanting you to venture out of your small and safe circle, to experience different things to broaden your horizons. It might just be your yolk wanting to be cultivated so you can get back into flow and balance.

These are the questions to ask yourself to usher in change and growth. Too many of us are stuck in a rut and don't even ask the questions. I think it's time to start asking. Are you making time in your day to get outdoors, into the fresh air? Do you feel better after being out in nature? Does it help you feel more centred and calmer? Does it give you inspiration and ideas to fuel your creative fire? Is it something you need to address?

Only *you* can cultivate your own yolk; I hope this book is your catalyst.

The story of Jim

My grandfather Jim was a strong, loving man who worked hard to provide for his family. Jim had a difficult upbringing, born to a single mother in wartime with a father who went off to war and never made it home. Jim never really had the anchor of a stable family and home life. He never knew his father, and never had the foundations that most families provide. He was somewhat of a lost soul, longing for stability and belonging.

His mother found a new home for Jim and herself when she married, and she went on to have more children as step siblings for Jim. But Jim never really felt he fit into this family, and did not see eye to eye with his stepfather. Jim was forced to leave home when he was 14 years old. He went to live with the family of his best friend. This family took Jim in and treated him with love and respect. He went on to marry Isobel, the sister of his best friend, and made a life for himself, his wife and his three young children.

Despite Jim's hard upbringing and tough shell, he possessed the softest of yolks, and was caring, steadfast, jovial and quietly devoted to his family. He did the best he could with what he had, and made the best of his circumstances. He always tried to be a good provider for his family.

It's my belief that Jim always strived to make a stable base to make up for this lack in his younger life. He was a carpenter, and seemed to want to build structures of permanence, to create this around him for his young family and for himself; he needed stability and strength and spent his life trying to achieve this.

Equally Jim needed nature and his garden; his years of being adrift and without a strong base made him feel at home in the garden, in nature, the place that belongs to anyone and everyone.

Jim loved roses. He loved to propagate them from cuttings and create the most beautiful blooms. His garden was filled with an array of heavily scented and multi-coloured roses, and they were his absolute pride and joy. It was as if he felt immense joy from creating something out of nothing. It reflected his journey, his story. To build something from nothing, to lay solid foundations.

I think that being out in nature, in the garden, cultivated my grandfather Jim's yolk. It soothed him and gave him joy. It tapped into the inside parts of him, the parts that were needing to heal from life's hurdles. Roses were his success story, a symbol of his own ability to prosper and grow despite the soil being less than perfect.

I always think of Jim whenever I see roses. I'm particularly drawn to that hybrid of pink and apricot, the rose that could be either colour. The way something of beauty has been meshed with different colours and different conditions, but survived and grown nonetheless. This to me resembles Jim, taking what he had in life and making something beautiful and permanent from it, despite the odds.

My husband bought me a bunch of beautiful pink roses for Valentine's Day one year and they instantly reminded me of my grandfather. I cut the stems and put the flowers in a vase, but didn't really tend to them. Still, they sat on my kitchen bench looking more perfect with every day that passed.

After two weeks, I was amazed to see my roses still looked picture perfect. The buds had opened into full, perfumed blooms and stood perfect and still on my kitchen bench. I sent a photo on my phone to the local florist to tell her how well they had lasted.

Another two weeks elapsed and I realised my roses were still looking beautiful. I started to think there was a little bit of magic unfolding right there in my kitchen. My roses were defying the odds and surviving despite the conditions. They had a strange sense of permanence about them, like they would continue to withstand the natural challenges and odds against them. I could not help but draw an analogy to my grandfather Jim and the way he lived his life. He tried to create that sense of permanence, with his carpentry and building, with his roses and his garden. He cultivated his yolk doing the things that brought him joy, that healed him and soothed his soul. He carried on with his life, finding his moments of joy and pleasure despite the odds.

My four-week-old roses were his tribute, his legacy, his permanence. They were a magical reminder to me of his ever presence in my life, in the small things; the flowers, the garden, the scents and colours. They were a reminder for me to find the time to 'smell the roses', to find time to heal and to find joy in the simple pleasures. They were a reminder for me to cultivate my yolk every single chance I could.

Many people tell me of their personal connection to certain flowers; they remind them of loved ones no longer with us. May I say to you that your loved ones live on in the beauty of those flowers, in their scent, colour and beauty. They have permanence, and so do your memories.

CREATIVITY

I believe creativity is a way of expressing and cultivating the hidden talents and abilities in our yolks. Creativity allows us to sync into the natural flow of life and be 'in the moment'. Many of us know the wonderful feeling of losing all sense of time and place when immersed in a creative pursuit. To be writing and let the words fall onto the page. To be painting and the brush just leads the way. To be gardening and be immersed in the scent and the beauty of nature. To be playing music that stirs the soul. To sing from the depths of within and get lost in the melody. To cook and delight in the aromas and textures.

Every one of us has an affinity with a particular creative pursuit that draws us in and feeds the soul. Something we enjoy, something that stirs us and drives us emotionally. Something that awakens dormant talent waiting to be birthed from our yolks. We all know this. We just have to tap into it and – most importantly – find time for it in our busy lives. To be lost in a creative task enables us to be present, for future and past to fall away so talents we were born with rise to the surface.

Creativity can quiet the mind but also awaken it. It creates flow and energy and stirs ideas and potential. Creativity tugs on the central thread into which all our parts are interwoven. It ignites a flame, it stirs the pot of stagnant energy. It centres us in the now and the task at hand.

How many of us talk about doing things that are 'good for the soul'? That make life worth living, that take us off the relentless treadmill of routine and expose us to new ways of being? How many of us prioritise careers and making a dollar over creative pursuits which would enrich our lives and use our unique talents?

CULTIVATING YOUR YOLK

Creativity cultivates our yolks. It has cultivated mine through the delicate unfolding of writing this book.

Creativity has a magical ripple effect; we all can benefit from hearing each other sing or listening to a beautifully composed piece of music. We all can feel moved by reading a heartfelt poem or story, or be lost in the colours of a majestic painting. We all can enjoy the scent of a beautifully manicured garden or delight in the tastes and smells of a lovingly prepared meal.

Pleasure is gained by the giver and the receiver. Everyone wins, and so the cycle of giving and receiving prevails. Creative pursuits have the potential to evoke the magic within us all, tapping into something sitting dormant but just waiting to come to life.

Reality television is full of cooking competitions, physical challenges, talent competitions and the like. They have the ability to draw us in as they can connect us to our own hidden talents and skills lying dormant beneath our shells. How often do we hear our friends and family say they could never go on those shows because they fear judgement? How many of us sit in front of our television screens judging those who have taken a leap of faith to pursue their creative passions? So often we see the contestants cry and see raw emotion displayed because exposing our yolks takes courage. It's easier to stay small and sheltered inside our shells of fear than to crack them wide open and pursue our dreams. But is it a life well lived? Is it utilising the yolk's potential and the talents gifted to us at birth? Remember it is the cracks where the light gets in to ignite us.

Some would argue that those who aren't good at a particular talent should not waste time pursuing and expressing it. That the less skilled singers should not be on the singing shows or in the choir. I disagree. It's not anything to do with judgement. It's about unique expression. To 'lose yourself' in a song, singing from the depths of your heart, is a beautiful thing to witness. The few notes off key go unnoticed, as we can be swept up in the emotion of someone expressing their yolk, their talents.

When we lose ourselves in a creative expression, we are formless. We lose the shell. We become the song. We become the music. Time stands still and we are lost in the moment. These moments of unique creative expression are magnificent. We need more of them in our lives.

The expression of our yolks feels liberating, feels right, deep within us. It enables life to flow through us. It validates, nurtures and supports us. Creative self-expression is our gift to ourselves, the food for our souls. After all, we are on this earth to express who we are. That is the whole point of our lives and what we *should* be doing.

Creativity ignites happiness within us. There are so many avenues of creativity available to explore in our lifetime. Supporting ourselves equates to enabling ourselves to find the right fit. Trial and error. Seek and find. There are no limitations, only possibilities when we step out of our own way. When we let the shell fall away, let down our guard and step into our own light.

We can all pledge to love ourselves enough to find the time to set aside for creativity in our lives. Imagine what we could explore and what opportunities would be available to us in the absence of fear. Imagine the joy that could be infused into life by following our intuition and allowing the creative juices to flow. Imagine if we loved ourselves so much that we chose to cultivate our yolks every day and schedule time for creativity.

We are all here to transcend our limitations and recognise the talents of our yolks. Unless we are happy with ourselves, we will not be happy with everything around us, including what we do.

Giving ourselves permission and time to be creative enables us to be happy, and then other things fall into place. When we are happy, we are more content with what we do, what we have and who we are surrounded by.

Creativity allows us to better discover who we are, to discover our yolks. It helps us to align with our gifts and talents. Simply slowing down in order to paint or garden lessens the pace and urgency of everything around us. It helps us to be more grounded and centred. It is in that space that we can just be; be content and present.

Creativity and creative pursuits such as art are now seen as forms of therapy. Art therapy allows creative expression to facilitate healing. When we anchor ourselves in the present, we can feel joy, we can be happy. Creating a piece of art can enhance wellbeing. Picasso said, 'Art washes away from the soul the dust of everyday life'.

Creating a piece of art can also give the artist insight into themselves, as the art may represent themes or issues which have risen to the surface and are portrayed in the art. The quietening of the mind and the presence required to be still opens the gateway for these insights to be revealed.

We can learn a lot about ourselves from our art and benefit enormously from the practice. We can all be open to the greater awareness of knowing we need creative expression in our busy lives, to discover and reveal our yolks, to get in touch with our true selves.

Ask yourself … are you making time to light your creative fire?

What creative skills are just waiting to surface? What creations are wanting to be birthed?

What stands in your way? Only you, my friend … only you.

GIVING

Giving is the act of providing for another, whether that gift be love, care, money or time. The act of giving cultivates our yolks and enables us to be of service for others, which facilitates connection. I believe we need a balance of giving and receiving; outflow is needed as equally as inflow, in order to thrive.

As a woman and a mother, I'm constantly aware of feeling like I'm giving too much to my family and children. When I cater too much to their needs and not to my own, I feel unbalanced and a bit grumpy. I now know that self-care is so important, and that if I look after my own needs and feel content then my family benefits from my happier state. I create a ripple effect of happier energy in my home.

Conversely, if we lead our lives constantly looking to receive, we are also out of balance. We need balance: giving and receiving. Giving is hardwired into our systems, our DNA. We feel good when we give, when we give of ourselves to benefit others. It tugs at our very core and cultivates our yolks. It helps us to tune into the deepest parts of ourselves.

True fulfilment and meaning come from impacting positively on the lives of others, and giving creates this impact.

The act of giving without expecting anything in return actually helps us to create balance, for when we give with no expectations it opens the floodgates for us to receive. It's like life works in our favour to balance out our good deed. We benefit from giving and feeling good about ourselves. We help others through our giving, and are rewarded by opening up to the flow of receiving.

So many times in my life when I have given my time, my energy, my talents, I have been so uplifted by what I unexpectedly received

CULTIVATING YOUR YOLK

in return. It might be the heartfelt thanks and love I feel projected back to me. I've had so many occasions when giving has really cultivated my yolk. It has felt like I have won the lottery; I have felt an outpouring of gratitude directed back at me.

I felt this sense of gratitude in writing this book. I felt that baring my yolk and revealing myself was giving of myself so that others might benefit. I just had to work through the vulnerability and fear.

Those feelings, those moments are what we all long for. It's what cultivates us. It's what truly connects us to the deepest versions of ourselves, as giving back enables us to take a positive step to living in alignment with our yolks.

When we are rushing around trying to acquire and receive, we are living a life that's not aligned. When we gain fulfilment from reaching out, helping and giving back, we bring ourselves back into balance. The struggle of trying to attain things diminishes and our focus is removed from ourselves and directed towards others. When we ask ourselves how we can give back we are acknowledging we have enough ourselves, that our supply is abundant and we have plenty to share.

It is a very subtle but powerful shift that takes place in our minds. It shifts our gears into a state of gratitude. It shifts our focus off ourselves and onto others. When we focus on others and how we can impact on their lives, we connect. We connect with our own yolks and then with theirs. Once again, we are brought back to the truth that we are all inextricably connected, all for the common good, all serving each other, all giving and receiving from the one collective source. From that collective source everyone's needs can be met, as there is an over-abundant supply. It's just about circulating it all around, balancing it all with equal measure, giving and receiving.

All we have to do is get in sync. Start giving and watch how life opens up. We all have a need to be of service, to help, to feel valued.

We all know family or friends who won't reveal their yolks, won't expose their vulnerabilities, won't let us past their shells. They don't let us truly help them when they are in need, due to fear, pride or vulnerability. They keep the walls up; perhaps they see this as brave or strong, or perhaps they feel they are less of a burden. But they do us and themselves a great disservice, as the act of giving helps us to cultivate the best parts of us. When people shut us out, we cannot help, we cannot be of service. We inadvertently can disconnect from those we are trying to help. If they dropped the armour and revealed their vulnerabilities, we would have greater connection.

So, ask yourself these questions: are you finding time to give back, to be of service to others? Do you feel it could help to cultivate your best parts? Do you feel it could help you to leave your footprint, your legacy in this one life you have?

I would love you to really think about that as you read about William and Connie, two remarkable individuals who gave so much. I think their acts of giving became their legacies, and I am so honoured to share their stories.

The story of William and Connie

My stories of William and Connie illustrate the amazing qualities of two extraordinary people who both expressed the true essence of giving; in their short lifetimes, they cultivated their yolks by being of service to others. These stories also demonstrate an amazing interconnection and the incredible synchronicities at play to bring me to this point to share them.

Earlier I introduced my wonderful grandfather, Jim, a man who never knew his father due to the hardships of war. Jim's father was a man named William, a merchant from St Arnaud, Victoria, who enlisted in the ultimate act of giving and went off to fight for his country. William was a lance corporal of the 57th Battalion, which fought in the small rural village of Passchendaele in Belgium in World War I – 38,000 Australians became casualties in this small village and never made it home to their loved ones. William was one of those, killed in action on 26 October 1917. He never got to know his son Jim, and sacrificed his life to protect his country.

I feel as I write about a great grandfather I never knew that I am honouring him, honouring his short life and paying homage to a man whose life was in fact the greatest act of giving. I feel as if I am honouring his yolk.

My brother discovered the details about William's life and death through researching the family history and accessing Australian war records. He was trying to put the pieces of the puzzle together to share with the rest of the family. It was September 2017, and he knew it was nearing the 100-year anniversary of William's death.

I was meditating in the morning on 8 September 2017 when the word 'LYS' was channelled to me. I didn't understand the significance of the word at the time, but intuitively I knew it was in reference to William. I then felt the strong sense of my great grandfather William, dressed in his battered army uniform with a ripped, bloodied area above his heart. He looked of similar build and colouring to Paul, the brother who was researching William's life. He was medium height with pale, freckled skin, hairy arms and dark hair. He was showing me the wound to his heart, which represented his sadness of never getting to know his now large extended family.

William's son Jim spent his life trying to cultivate strong family connections, to compensate for him not having this as a child. William showed me his sadness that he never had the opportunity to experience being a father and raising a family. It was incredibly emotional to connect with William and feel his lost hopes and dreams.

I then went on to investigate the significance of the word LYS, and learnt that the Battle of the Lys occurred not long after William's death, and was in a region very close to Passchendaele, in Belgium. Lys was the name of the river that crossed the zone where many of the battles took place.

I rang my brother and told him of my discovery, and we used this information to piece together another fragment that helped us understand William's life.

The next day I was scrolling through a social media site and was drawn to the sad story of the passing of Constance Johnson, a beautiful young mother who had died of cancer. Connie, as she was known, had suffered from bone cancer as a child, uterine cancer as a young woman, and finally succumbed to breast cancer at age 40. Connie was the sister of actor Samuel Johnson, who is well loved and known in Australia.

Connie and her brother founded the Love Your Sister charity in 2012, with the aim of raising $10 million for cancer research. Connie's later years were spent trying to give back, to help others find a cure for cancer. She was awarded the Medal of the Order of Australia on 7 September and died the following day.

I was overcome with sadness while reading a heartfelt post by Samuel about Connie's passing. As I read through his beautiful tribute, I stopped in shock at the word LYS, in reference to their charity. I was dumbstruck; it was the same word given to me while mediating and channelling.

I immediately went to my bedroom and got my journal out from the bedside drawer. I realised I had written the word LYS in my journal on 8 September, the actual date of Connie's passing.

I was so amazed by the synchronicity of events that had linked William's and Connie's stories together. I could not help but see the correlation between these two beautiful people who had given so much to be of service to others.

Fifteen days later I was reading the newspaper when I turned the page and was again completely dumbstruck to see an article and photo of Connie and Samuel on the left-hand side of the page and an article called 'Ghosts in the Field' on the right-hand side of the page. This article was describing the fallen soldiers from Ypres in Belgium, who died in September and October 1917, right near the river Lys, in the same month as William and in the same general location.

William and Connie are the most perfect examples of living a life of service, of giving to help others, of selfless acts of the most humble and loving nature. They are connected stories of two amazingly brave and giving individuals who were worlds apart while living, but eternally connected in the afterlife. They both cultivated their yolks in their short but meaningful lifetimes by being of service to others. In doing so their memories are so much brighter and their connection stronger. I'm the humble storyteller conveying their message, and I am inextricably connected to them both despite having never known them in their lifetimes. I have since received a message from Connie to her brother, and know that the universe will conspire for this to be delivered when the time is right.

I am incredibly honoured to share their stories, honour their beautiful yolks and illustrate the pieces of intrinsic magic that surround us all, every waking moment, if we venture to notice and believe.

Rest in peace William; rest in peace Connie.

RELATIONSHIPS

We all need to belong and need to be part of a tribe – it is hard-wired into our DNA.

It's no accident that we need both a male and female to produce a child. It is the first semblance of a tribe. It sets up the foundation of a family and of belonging. That is the most common basic framework to provide a nurturing and stable environment, though not the only one. We also know this structure is not always an assurance that those needs will be met. But the core elements of connection and belonging are paramount, no matter what people or genders make up that family unit.

We all desire to belong, feel loved and be surrounded by people who love our authentic selves. Research also supports the notion that loneliness is detrimental to health and longevity. In 2017, studies completed by the American Psychological Association found links between social isolation and a number of health risks. And studies at Brigham Young University found loneliness contributes to premature death. Good social connections support and assist us to thrive. A strong support network of family and friends helps us to be both happy and healthy.

We are all biologically programmed to connect and find both intimacy and support in relationships. Whether we choose to live with another or marry, we generally choose to be in a couple relationship so that intimacy is fostered. The key is to attain healthy, genuine relationships where we are unconditionally accepted for our yolks; where we are loved, supported and nurtured for who we are, without judgement or criticism. Relationships like these are our safe haven, as deep within our yolks we all crave love, belonging and human connection.

Sometimes we have to ask ourselves the hard questions and ascertain whether our relationships are receiving the attention they deserve. We have to pick apart the threads to really examine whether the relationships in our lives are supporting us or draining us. We have to evaluate whether our relationships are providing us the framework we need to feel secure and to be our best expression of ourselves.

It is often hard, at any life stage, to cut ties. There are often associated feelings of guilt when ending relationships, because it's difficult for us to put our own needs first. It can be hard to let go of what is no longer serving us. But ultimately, we need to be surrounded by people who love and accept our authentic selves.

Family relationships are often fraught with difficulties as we cannot always sever ties just because we don't feel acceptance, love or security. We can choose other relationships in our lives but we do not get to choose our families.

I believe we are meant to have the different blend of family members for our own learnings and growth. This doesn't mean it's an easy ride; it can often be a difficult road to navigate, but I believe we are all meant to be on that road for the long haul and the binds of family often ensure that.

It's imperative to examine the relationships in our lives and start asking the questions to ascertain if they are serving our yolks, and our growth.

So, start asking yourself the questions …

The story of Louise and Rayya

Sometimes relationships are so powerful in life that they transcend the space between life and the afterlife; they remain the same, untouched by death.

One morning I was meditating and channelling when I received a unique message, almost like a code. It was given to me by Louise Hay.

I am a late follower of Louise Hay as my journey of personal development took some time to develop momentum. In the last few years I have read hundreds of books on personal development, healing, metaphysics, spirituality, health, wellness and mindfulness. However, the books that spoke most directly to my yolk were those written by Louise Hay. I have felt the most strange and surreal connection to her and to her teachings. When I have watched videos of Louise speaking and lecturing, I have almost felt like I was watching an older version of myself.

It feels vulnerable to admit, but nonetheless truthful: Louise often comes to me when I am meditating and provides me with the most wonderful advice and guidance. On this particular day – Australia Day, 26 January – Louise instructed me to write a code in my journal.

It said: '1 2 3 You are me'.

The symbolism of the message was to encourage me to keep writing and helping to heal people with my words, my message, my book, just as she had in her lifetime. She told me she was of a similar age when she wrote her first book. The message was incredibly profound as it was illustrating the power of connection, that death was no barrier to connection, and that although

I never knew Louise when she was alive, I could still have connection and guidance from her in spirit.

Two days later, I was scrolling through Instagram when I came across a photo of Elizabeth Gilbert, an author whom I follow and greatly admire. She was holding a piece of paper saying '1 2 3'. She had found this note in her desk drawer and had no idea as to why she had written it. She was asking if anyone knew its meaning.

I was quite taken aback seeing this message, and felt it was part of some magical weave of interconnection. I knew Elizabeth had recently lost her life partner and soul mate Rayya, and I had often felt a very strong sense of Rayya whenever Elizabeth posted a comment about her loss and grief. I knew the universe was up to some kind of big magic but couldn't quite work out all the missing pieces of the puzzle.

I decided to go for a walk to clear my head and talk to my husband about the strange set of events. As I was walking, I remembered a previous post from Elizabeth, where she had intimated that Rayya still felt part of her, that she was Rayya and Rayya was her, almost like there was a meshing of their souls that could not be explained.

Then suddenly, with an amazing sense of clarity, I could here Rayya's voice saying, 'Don't you get it, 1 2 3 You are me!' I stopped in my tracks, realising the message, the code was for Elizabeth and myself, a message sent to me and meant for Elizabeth, a stranger, living on the other side of the globe.

As I stopped, I looked upwards to see I was standing right below a big, beautiful kookaburra sitting on the power lines. I immediately realised my message from Louise arrived on Australia Day. I instantly saw the connection of the kookaburra and Rayya's words to me. I knew it was both unusual to see a kookaburra in the inner-city streets of Melbourne and that the timing of its appearance was exactly at the time I heard Rayya speak to me.

    I cannot begin to describe how profound the timing and sequencing of these events were for me. I cannot even begin to fathom how this crazy universe works, bringing people together, conspiring to connect, uplift, heal and comfort complete strangers on opposite sides of the planet. I do not think any of us quite comprehend the big magic and mystery of this world we inhabit, and how treasured relationships between two people can survive and thrive across dimensions, barriers, times and ages. I am in awe of life and all its beautiful secrets, and honoured to share some of its mysteries with you.

    May all of your special relationships be as magical as the one shared between Elizabeth and Rayya.

HEALTH

So much research today is pointing to the mind–body connection, with pioneers in the field such as Louise Hay and Dr Joe Dispenza leading the way. Research now supports that not only do we need physical health, we also need emotional and spiritual health. Studies by Shin et al, for example, confirm the benefits of physical exercise improving mental health, and multiple other studies support the connection between physical and mental health. We are beings of balance, and a healthy mind can assist to produce a healthy body. We need adequate sleep to repair and rejuvenate, so our cells repair while we rest. We know we need to remain physically active, and that regular exercise promotes health and wellbeing. As a Physiotherapist and a Pilates Instructor I have engaged in physical exercise for most of my life, and definitely feel the benefits.

We agree that achieving a balance of restful sleep and physical activity is important to maintain health. We also require good nutrition and a balanced diet to promote optimal heath, keeping sugar to a minimum and upping our intakes of vegetables and fruit.

For me personally, from my work and the hundreds of books I have read and studied on heath, I believe there are five non-negotiables to improve nutrition and health:

- eat more vegetables and fruit
- limit sugar
- maintain hydration by drinking lots of water
- remain physically active
- get adequate sleep.

CULTIVATING YOUR YOLK

We all know that if we support our physical health by eating well, getting a good night's sleep and exercising, we *feel* better. It supports our body, and it supports our emotional health too. Our heads are clearer, we feel less brain fog, we have more energy, and we generally feel happier and more balanced.

It's my belief that everything in our bodies is so intertwined and everything craves a unified state of balance. We want a healthy lifestyle to support this overall balance: restful sleep, good nutrition and regular exercise. Just as we need downtime with meditation, we need uptime with physical exercise. Every component of how we live our lives affects the health of our minds and our bodies. Any practice that enables us to quieten the busy mind and focus has the potential to cultivate the yolk to achieve a unified state of balance.

For me, Pilates has been my saving grace and my personal way of focusing on my core, literally and metaphorically. As a trained Physiotherapist I have taught Pilates and practised it for many years. The process of focusing inward and activating different muscle groups makes me present and anchored. It quietens my mind without the adrenaline and cortisol response of cardiovascular exercise. For me it is restorative exercise, as it is for countless others as well.

Pilates is my personal favourite as it provides me with spinal stability, needed due to an old back injury and problems that arose from a difficult epidural during labour. For many, yoga is their go-to and provides the same restorative blend of exercise that calms the central nervous system and facilitates balance.

It is no surprise to me that my physical balance has improved with Pilates, and that has led to a greater feeling of overall balance. I honestly never felt that with other forms of more intensive exercise, many of which I have trialled over a long career in physiotherapy and fitness. While I have no doubt that fitness training and cardio-type exercise programs are good for cardio fitness, they are not always good for restoration and balance.

Over the course of my career working with many women, I have seen the drive for women to push their bodies to get results; to get fit, lose weight and improve their body shape. Nearly all of the emphasis is on chasing something they don't have; the correct weight, the perfect shape, the right dress size, the best level of fitness.

I get it. I've been there a thousand times over. And I have come to one massive realisation: if our female bodies detect something as even minutely stressful, we will have a stress response. We will burn sugar and store fat. We will switch to survival mode and have an adrenal gland response to produce cortisol.

Women are hardwired very differently to men, as we are cyclic; we ebb and flow. We are not static and stable; we have menstrual cycles and changes, pregnancies and menopause. Our hormone levels change on a daily basis, let alone throughout our lifetime. We are transient, and are therefore more finely tuned to changes in our bodies, and more altered by stressors.

I've heard so many stories of how women up the ante; they increase their exercise and decrease their calorie intake but don't see results on the scales. I have seen many premenopausal women worry about their changing bodies and recruit a boot camp–style personal trainer to push them even harder. In my experience it just doesn't work, as women need a balance.

Women need some form of restorative exercise, be it Pilates, yoga, walking in nature or Tai Chi. We need something to balance the ebb and flow, to stabilise us amid the changing, cyclic bodies we inhabit. Women need to be more mindful of self-restoration as they can often feel depleted by caring for everyone else's needs.

We are the caregivers, but we must give the care to ourselves first. We need to nurture ourselves as much as we nurture our families. Men I believe are more bulletproof and can weather the storms. They can fast and push their bodies harder. Their bodies don't appear to trigger as sensitively to the indicators of stress. They also benefit from restorative exercise. But women need and crave restoration, to calm the adrenal response to stress, to balance the ebb and flow. Attempts to push harder with cardio exercise and boot camp exercise regimes can often backfire, particularly at times when their bodies are undergoing change such as pregnancy or menopause.

Despite the type of exercise you subscribe to, restorative exercise has great benefits. It can help to quieten the busy mind, bring focus inward and help to achieve a better state of balance. Taking that gentle, restorative exercise outdoors is an added bonus. Connecting with nature and being outdoors is a great way to get grounded. The common denominators are about slowing down, looking inward and quietening the mind.

In that space we can cultivate our yolks.

I have also witnessed many women struggle to lose weight, change shape and improve fitness during different stages of life. Resistance to changing body shapes after having children is a big contributor to women feeling dissatisfied. Again, change and cycles are at play. Often women feel they just restore their weight to normal and then fall pregnant again. The ebb and flow fills our reproductive years. I witness many women struggling to achieve restoration after change. I see many women unhappy with their changing body shape.

'Struggle' and 'unhappy' are the two keywords.

It has taken me half my life to finally understand that what we resist ... persists. What we struggle with remains with us, like a noose around our necks. When we let go – let go of the struggle, accept ourselves, love ourselves, our size, our shape, our stretchmarks – the struggle dissolves. Because we as women are *meant to change*. We are meant to be cyclic and changing. We are not evergreen, we are deciduous. That's how we were made. That's how we roll ... and it's beautiful.

If we struggle and resist the change within, we deny ourselves self-acceptance as women. That is part of our beauty and part of our magic. Resisting our beautiful changes is resisting ourselves. We need to embrace change and view ourselves in a whole new light. We need to be in awe of our amazing abilities to change, grow, give birth, restore, cycle, ebb and flow. We need to love ourselves unconditionally through every cycle.

Through puberty, pregnancy and menopause, through thick and thin, up and down, fat or thin. We need to love our yolks. The parts of us that make us authentically beautiful and real. We need to embrace all parts of us wholeheartedly and unconditionally. Not just love ourselves, with conditions; when we weigh a certain amount, when we fit a certain dress size, when we are fit, when we are slim.

Love is the answer. Self-love is the solution. Love our yolks, pure and simple. Abolish the conditions. Who made those rules? We don't have to fit any criteria in order to be loved, especially by *ourselves*. We need to stop being our own worst critic and start being our own number one supporter. We need to join our own fan club, not in a narcissistic way but in a healthy dose of 'self-love' kind of way. We need to find the time to cultivate that self-love, doing the things that make us feel it.

But the noise of our too-busy lives has muted our inner voices that are pleading for some self-love, some me time, some R and R, some food for the soul.

We all know this strikes a chord deep inside.

So, what are we going to do about it?

I hope you might be comforted by reading the story of Ella, a caring and devoted grandmother who was able to help her granddaughter achieve better health from the other side.

The story of Ella

My close friend lost her mother Ella a few years ago. Ella was a small-statured, quietly spoken lady, and her yolk was caring, wise and kind. Her strength belied her small frame, as she was born and raised in the country and in a generation that worked hard and soldiered on through adversity.

Ella lost her husband when she was young and raising a family. She managed to raise her children with a quiet strength and dignity, and lived to the remarkable age of 92.

My friend found the loss of her mother particularly difficult, as did her children. Ella was like the sun around which all the family orbited, and her absence made them feel somewhat in the shadows.

I was having dinner at my friend's house and we were chatting about her daughter's health. My friend had told me she had found herself in a bookshop and was particularly drawn to purchase a book titled *Deliciously Ella*. She felt the name was in reference to her own mother, and felt Ella was urging her to buy the book.

She purchased two copies; one for her daughter and one for herself. Her daughter had been experiencing some issues with her heart, and the doctors were struggling to find the cause.

My intuition told me her heart issues were partly attributed to the grief in her heart; the grief felt for her grandmother's passing. I thought she would benefit from seeing a kinesiologist and a wholistic medicine practitioner.

My friend had given her daughter the book after returning from the store. Her daughter took it to her room and began flipping through the introduction.

CULTIVATING YOUR YOLK

She returned in tears to talk to her mother. On reading about the story of Ella in the book it was discovered that the author had exactly the same heart condition. She had learnt to heal her health issues with dietary changes and the healing properties of a plant-based diet. Both my friend and her daughter knew that Ella, the mother and grandmother, had guided them to this book as a way to help the daughter heal.

My friend relayed this beautiful story to me, and I told her that I in fact was a follower of 'deliciously Ella' and had bought another one of her books. She was amazed I had heard of this author and wellness advocate, and was surprised by the synchronicity of events. I suggested to her that her daughter would also benefit from visiting a kinesiologist to further help her to heal. I promised to send her the details of a practitioner the next day.

As a beautiful gesture my friend gave me her own copy of the book as I was leaving. She felt so happy that her daughter was on the right path to healing. I was incredibly touched to receive this gift.

That night before I drifted off to sleep my thoughts were of my friend and her beautiful daughter. I had a very vivid dream. Ella, my friend's mother, came to me in a dream. She gently opened my hand and put one blue butterfly onto the palm of my hand. She told me the blue butterfly was for her granddaughter, just for her. I woke up and was amazed by the clarity of my dream and the specifics of it. This wasn't just any coloured butterfly. It was specifically blue and just for her granddaughter.

I was prompted to call my friend to thank her for a lovely dinner and also for my beautiful book, but I thought I should first find the details of the kinesiologist for her. I'd been to a practitioner before that I wanted to recommend, but I couldn't remember the name of the business. I searched online, and to my amazement, when I found the business the name was … Blue Butterfly Kinesiology.

I was stunned. My intuition had told me the daughter would benefit from seeing the kinesiologist and my dream had further shown me I was on the right path. I rang my friend and told her about my dream.

Ella had given guidance on the book to buy and the practitioner to visit. She was still guiding her family and helping them cultivate their yolks, all from spirit. All the wonderful qualities of Ella's yolk – her wisdom, her insight, her intelligence and devotion – lived on. She was still present and assisting her family. My friend had been finding it hard to lift her spirits in her mum's absence, and this series of events really helped to lessen her sadness and fill her with hope.

A few days later I was in my garden when I saw a white butterfly lying outstretched on the step to my back door. I gently picked it up and put it on a plant in my garden and went back inside. Soon after, some friends came over. On this particular morning I was wearing a blue singlet. My friends walked into the house and started saying, 'You are the butterfly lady!' I looked at them, puzzled. 'Look at your chest … there's a butterfly on it!' To my amazement the butterfly I had picked up from the step was resting on my chest above my heart in the same open-winged position. My friend took a photo of it. The butterfly stayed in this position for at least 20 minutes.

I decided to send the photo of the butterfly to my friend, saying that I thought Ella was still making her presence felt. I asked my friend if she had booked the appointment for her daughter.

CULTIVATING YOUR YOLK

At that exact moment in time my friend was driving past my house and thought to herself she must book the appointment for her daughter. As she thought this her phone made a sound as the photo of the butterfly was delivered. As she glanced quickly to her phone, she saw the image of the butterfly resting on my chest above the blue singlet.

So many events and synchronicities could only be the guidance of my friend's mother Ella. She was helping her granddaughter cultivate her yolk and find the answers to improve her health and wellness. It's inspiring and amazing to realise we are able to access this love and guidance from our loved ones in spirit. We just need to connect and be open to the signs.

I have so many wonderful and awe-inspiring moments like this occur and it fills me with hope and wonder. I get to see the miracles at play all around me every moment. These moments remind me of the absolutely extraordinary world we live in, and the even more extraordinary space we inhabit once we pass over. It's clear that everything and everyone remains interconnected and interwoven at the deepest level. How those we lose are never truly lost to us. How the circle of life is a never-ending, revolving circle of love and support.

It is an absolute joy to me that I'm reminded of this wonder, and that I get to share these remarkable and inspiring stories. It is truly the biggest gift and I am so very grateful for it.

SPIRITUALITY

Cultivating ourselves and our yolks requires a multifaceted approach. We need to have healthy emotional lives, healthy physical lives, healthy relationships, healthy spiritual lives.

We need all pieces of the pie to balance us out. Being in tune with our yolks enables us to be empowered and balanced. This state of connection facilitates the physical body manifesting health, the emotional body manifesting ease and the spiritual body manifesting balance. We can then tick all the boxes, sleep well, eat well and exercise. We can foster great relationships with friends and family. We can have creative outflow and a fully expressed life. We can squeeze in some meditation and give back a bit too.

But are we spiritually healthy? This is a last bit of the puzzle and quite often overlooked.

We all need to be spiritually fit, to have a healthy spiritual life; a life that connects us and gives us a sense of oneness with everyone and everything. It is the last step to cultivating our yolks and is essential to total health and wellness. A lot of people tune out when the concept of spirituality is discussed. For many it is wrapped up in layers of religious dogma. For others it seems far too in depth and a little confronting. It makes them uncomfortable and even a bit vulnerable expressing their beliefs on spirituality. It's just easier to avoid the topic. But avoiding it keeps us out of balance.

We have to ask ourselves, are we connected to the spiritual aspect of ourselves that moves us and uplifts us? That urges us on to break out and break free and be all we are meant to be? Are we in touch? Do we have a strong sense of self and purpose? Do we feel the common thread that binds us all together? Do we get the bigger picture at play which orchestrates everything for our growth and evolution? Do we feel connected to others and feel empathy and gratitude?

That to me is spiritual health, grassroots spirituality accessible to everyone despite their religious beliefs or persuasions, or lack of. It is not 'new age', it's common sense; it's what we all have the potential to feel, to access, to acquire.

It's the conversation we must have with ourselves to achieve spiritual fitness, so we are living in alignment with our yolks, with our truth. It forces us to go inward to our truth.

Spiritual health and wellbeing keep us anchored to our yolks, connected and in touch. Without that anchor it is easier for anxiety, unhappiness, negativity and despair to creep in. It is easier to lose centre. It is easier to veer off track and feel lost and despondent. To grow and evolve we need to look after the physical, the emotional and the spiritual parts of us. Only then will we achieve balance.

When we are spiritually healthy, we are aligned with the energy field of infinite possibility and potential. We just have to match our vibration and lift our emotional state to whatever it is we dream of and then act as if we have already achieved it. We all have a hunch that positive thoughts can create positive outcomes. We all have potentially at least once in our lifetimes put those positive vibes out there and felt them come back to us. We all have such an unlimited source of potential and possibility surrounding us just waiting to be accessed. Once we get clear on what we truly desire and dare to dream of our potential realised, then we need to match our emotions to the state of feeling our dreams are realised.

We are the only ones standing in our own way.

So, ask yourself, what do *you* need to change to address the basic needs of your yolk?

Do you need to support your physical health, eat better, and abolish some unhealthy habits and addictions that are not serving you?

Do you need to get better sleep and more physical exercise?

Do you need to find the pursuit that lights your creative fire and then find the time to do it?

Do you need to find loving, authentic relationships with people who accept you in all your glory and love you unconditionally?

Do you need to rid yourself of toxic relationships?

Do you need to address your emotional needs and find more happiness and gratitude and feel less stressed and rushed?

You already know the answers. You know what you need to do to truly cultivate that big, beautiful yolk of yours; to get you back in touch with *you;* to find yourself, find your balance again.

What needs to be done? What are you waiting for? Life is meant to be lived to its fullest potential. You are meant to be happy and loved and enjoy the journey you are on. Happiness is your birthright. You just have to decide what needs to be done, then start being it.

Get to it. Start cultivating your yolk and start *being* who you are meant to be. You can have loads of money, a great career, healthy relationships and lots of friends but you still need the last piece of the puzzle to be really happy. You need to check in, listen and do what feels right. You need to trust your intuition and stop pushing away or ignoring the messages it gives you.

YOLK PRACTICES

List 1: Cultivate your yolk

STRETCH

Write a list of every way you are cultivating your yolk, in regards to health, relationships, giving back, finding time in nature, meditating, creative pursuits and so on.

List 2: What does your yolk want you to change?

What's missing? What do you need *more of* in your life to feel more balanced? What do you need *less of?* What needs to be addressed, removed, enhanced or improved? What is no longer serving you?

You know the answers. Write them down and see them on paper in front of you.

The categories are already talking to you, trying to get your attention.

Your body has already been giving you signals and alerts for some time now and you have not been paying them the attention they require.

You know it. I know it.

This book found you. Not the other way around. It found you for a reason.

So, look at the categories and write your list in your journal. Write down what needs addressing:

- mindfulness
- nature

- creativity
- giving
- relationships
- health
- spirituality.

Make an *action* list. Who do you need to help you?

What do you need to do to start turning it all around?

Put it out there; get started. If you are new to meditation, give it a go. Visit my website Bernadettesomers.com to access your free Yolk Meditation. Trial it every day for a month and see how you feel, see the shifts. I promise you that it is infused with spirit's help to help you get connected from the inside out.

You have nothing to lose and so much to gain – so please try it.

Journey Home

May the butterflies guide you on your way home.
May you go safely whilst the owl stands guard.
May you carry the piece of my heart that remains yours.
May the stars guide me to a place of surrender.
May your memory shine brighter than the sun.
May you rest eternally nestled in my love.

BERNADETTE SOMERS

6. The everlasting yolk

THIS CHAPTER FALLS near the end of my book for a reason. Chapter by chapter we have chipped away our shells together, both you the reader and me the writer. It's been a gentle and delicate unfolding, as all learning should be, so that the wisdom of the learnings is set in place. It is no irony that the book itself reveals its own majestic yolk, its heart and soul, in this chapter.

I hope you have travelled the pages of the book through the code of loving, expressing and cultivating your yolk and absorbed the magic of the stories of the everlasting yolks.

The difficulty in discussing the everlasting yolk, or life after death, is that we have no factual proof. We have many stories and themes from those who have experienced near-death experiences. We have spiritual mentors and authors expressing their beliefs and theories. But until we all individually pass over we will not fully grasp the truth about life after death.

Nearly all religious codes refer to the afterlife, as it is a belief that gives many hope. Hope is often what we cling to; it gives us comfort as we approach our final days. It also gives us solace when we lose a loved one. Some would argue we all have a vested interest in believing there is something else to look forward to, a life in the spiritual realm after we die a physical death.

It is fair to say that most of you reading this book will have experienced the loss of a loved one. We recognise grief can surface at any given moment despite having experienced a loss many years prior. The emotions can feel intense and raw, and the sense of loss profound. Grief is the stranger that visits whenever he chooses. Emotions can spill over at the most inopportune times and with no warning. Grief is universal and it strips us bare.

Death is inevitable. It's the club we all have membership to. Most of us fear death and dying. We see it as an end with nothing tangible after it. Those in their twilight years carry the reality that it's closer than they would like. However, I believe with every fibre of my being that death is *not* the end. I believe we are born with our yolks, and we leave with them too. We lose our shells and our physical bodies but our yolks are everlasting. They are made of energy and are filled with our essence and continue on. Our yolks are our pilot light that can never be extinguished. Our essence stays with us eternally.

I believe when we experience death, we lose our shells but maintain our yolks and continue on in spiritual form, in energy. We are still around but in a different dimension, a different energy. The limitations of the shell are just for this lifetime, not for eternity. The shell is just our temporary home; the yolk is all we take with us. This may help us to understand how to live – how to allow the yolk to transcend the shell, the limits, the body. The shell is the thing we need to get past to express our true selves. The shell is there to make us stretch, to challenge us, to enable us to expand.

My life has been brightly coloured by a rainbow of experiences awakening me to the presence of those departed. For many years I've tried to reason and analyse the coincidences. I have doubted myself and doubted the messages received. I have resisted – but it has persisted. Now I have come to accept that even though I don't know the 'hows' and 'whys', I have an unwavering belief.

Over the course of my life, and particularly in the last few years when I have dropped the resistance, I've had so many signs from those who have passed on. Signs in the form of butterflies, birds, feathers, scents, numbers, dates. Signs like the beautiful stories woven through this book.

I have sensed, felt, heard, seen … and *known*.

I have no doubt. Only an unwavering certainty. Death is not the end. Our yolks live on. I will write another book with more stories relayed to me about other people sensing the presence of a departed loved one. It will be a collation of all these remarkable and inspiring stories.

#yolk_ _ _

I have sensed the energy and essence of a departed person without ever having known them when they were living. I describe their yolk to their loved ones, the beautiful core of who they were when living and still are now in spirit. It happens to me frequently and consistently, and I will forever be in awe of this magic.

I think of the yolk, the central, untainted essence of us living on and the withered shell falling away at our passing. For those of us who have had signs from departed loved ones, we can understand it better by drawing on this metaphor. We sensed their yolk. We have intuitively sensed them, thought of them, felt them, and felt comforted by them. We realise that what we remember, miss and love about them is actually their yolk. It's more than their memory, it's palpable and real.

So, with this truth I say there is less need for mourning. There is less sense of loss as our loved ones are still ever-present, still accessible. We can still access their yolks. We can still talk to them, and I believe they will hear. We can still feel their presence and still have connection. It is just a spiritual connection not a physical connection. It's available to us all if we believe. It's waiting. We are all just energy, whether it's in physical form while living or spiritual form after dying. Energy can be sensed and felt regardless. Energy remains with the yolk, the ever-present and everlasting yolk.

Our yolks keep us connected throughout life and after life. Death is no barrier to connection. It is just a changed state of being. Yolk to yolk, heart to heart, soul to soul, whatever you call it; it's real, it's accessible and it's truth. We take our yolks with us; they live on. Our essence, our unique expression lives on – it's our blueprint, our legacy.

So, I fill this chapter with more stories of people; some I knew in a physical life, and all of whom I've had the wonderful experience of connecting with after their departure. My stories are *their* stories, crafted by them. I'm just the humble storyteller. The stories serve to honour these people.

I hope these stories, and the stories woven through the book, resonate with people at their deepest core and tug at the strings of their faith in the unseen and unknown. They may stir some to ponder and reflect on their own stories of synchronicity. They may act as a catalyst to open the door for other occurrences. They may evoke a memory or recollection which may be also a message from spirit. It's my wish that their stories bring hope, solace and comfort. That this stirring creates a new way of viewing things that fills the hidden corners with a buoyancy of hope for the future. That we all find ourselves nestled in a new space of trust.

If you find yourself at this chapter of the book and you are longing to have similar connections as described in the stories woven through the pages, I say to you this.

You can.

You can follow this code.

You can start by connecting within, by loving your yolk. You can progress to braving fear and vulnerability to express your authentic self. You can do the Yolk Practices at the end of the main chapters.

This is your starting point, as it was mine. This is your guide to finding more connection in this life … and beyond.

Wings

Take your newfound wings and fly
High above us all
Go colour all our rainbows
Hear the angels call

To new and bright beginnings
To hope and love and light
To the warmth of a million sunsets
With no pain in sight

Where raindrops dilute all tears
And memories envelope us with love
Where love frees us to move forward
With you watching from above

BERNADETTE SOMERS

The story of Mark

My husband used to live with a great mate called Mark. He was quite a character; his yolk was funny, caring, loyal, giving and charming. He was small in stature but made up for it with loads of personality and charisma.

Mark was diagnosed with kidney cancer and had surgery and treatment to try to manage this illness. But the cancer was taking its toll.

In his last days, Mark called my husband to invite him over for a visit. He was weak and frail. He knew his days were numbered.

Upon arrival, Mark asked my husband to carry him to the car so they could go for a drive. He directed the way, knowing exactly where they were heading. They reached a lovely long driveway to a small cemetery lined with beautiful old trees. The tree branches were full with many black cockatoos that hailed their arrival with a chorus of cries.

My husband parked the car and helped his friend out. My husband helped Mark walk towards a clearing up ahead in the cemetery. From this vantage point there was a beautiful view of the countryside. Mark told my husband that it was the best view around and would be his final resting place. My husband was beyond words as he tried to process what his friend was telling him. They both sat on the grass taking in the majestic view with moments of banter and moments of complete silence.

My husband opened up and told Mark about his experience at his father's grave where the magpies had given him a sign his father was watching over. Mark grinned, acknowledging the wonder of the story, and said to my husband he would like to do something like that when it was his turn.

The two friends spent an hour or two at the cemetery, enjoying what would be their last time together.

Mark's funeral was a true celebration of his life. He orchestrated the details of his send off to represent the way in which he lived his life; with fun and with joy. He wrote his own eulogy and chose all his favourite songs to be played. During the eulogy he asked everyone to turn and say hello to whomever was sitting next to them, as they were his friends and worth getting to know. The service was uplifting and joyous despite the sadness. It was littered with many jokes and many laughs.

My mother had come over to babysit our small children so we could attend the funeral. When we retuned, I was at the front of the house when I heard my mother calling out, 'Shoo … shoo'. Puzzled, I went to the back of the house to see what the commotion was. As I walked towards my mother, I saw a small magpie-lark walking down the hallway towards my husband and me. Somehow the magpie-lark had entered the house and was quite a few metres from the doorway.

I locked eyes with my husband as we both uttered the same word: 'Mark.' We both just *knew*. We knew without a shadow of a doubt that this was his sign to us; this was his way of showing us he was still watching over.

It was one of those incredible moments that renders us speechless: a moment that leaves us in awe and wonder. A moment that shakes us awake and reminds us there are forces at play which we don't quite understand. To remind us we are all individual threads in a huge and intricate tapestry woven together to connect us all.

THE EVERLASTING YOLK

These moments take our breath. They remind us that beyond our physical lives lies another dimension, one which is hard to define but is nevertheless real. It gives us comfort. It gives us hope. It helps us to not fear death, and to believe death is not the end, it just delivers us to a new beginning.

Departure

Butterflies circle in a dance of love
Lifting my spirit to soar
Could there be a blue more vivid?
Than the sky I share with you

Flowers bloom to the beat of my heart
I am buoyant with the scent
The music of my soul plays unannounced
Awakening me to the unfolding joy

Can I share with you the beauty of
What resides within
Pure and uniquely mine
Allow me to scatter my petals
Before I depart
To forever … linger …

BERNADETTE SOMERS

The story of Nell

Several years ago, my cousin and my dear friend's grandmother passed away. Nell was a very gentle and quiet lady. Her yolk was very wise, kind and thoughtful and her love was unwavering. She was small and fine in stature, but despite this she anchored the entire family with a quiet strength and composure.

Nell was quiet and measured while living, but seemed to be so much stronger and forthright in spirit. Her three granddaughters felt a strong connection to her and often asked her for guidance and support.

My cousin and I are lifelong friends and share a wonderfully close bond. We're part of a very large family who all love to laugh and enjoy getting together. Every year we have a big Christmas catch up where we dance the night away and enjoy the togetherness.

On this particular day I was meditating in the afternoon before the event. I felt Nell make her presence known and come through to deliver a message for my cousin. I write down everything that is conveyed to me to pass on the message accurately. Nell had a beautiful and personal message for my cousin about finding love. I asked Nell to give me some sort of sign to validate her message. I find this always helps the recipient to truly believe in the message and take heed of the wise words. Nell showed me an image and instructed me to draw it.

It looked like a microphone; a round top with a thin handle below. She asked me to colour it with red-and-white stripes. I truly had no idea what I was drawing but did as instructed. I trusted it would show up as required to validate her message to her granddaughter. She told me to tell her granddaughter to dance like nobody is watching and sing into the microphone-shaped object.

Later that evening I spoke to my cousin and told her I had a beautiful message for her from her grandmother. I didn't want to get into a deep and meaningful conversation early in the night as we were both there to have fun. So, I just briefly mentioned the sign I was given in the form of the red-and-white-striped object. Neither of us knew what it meant or what the object was.

The family gathering got into full force with everyone dancing and singing. Later in the night I found myself dancing next to my cousin. We were having so much fun, and were singing along to the music. We were singing at the top of our voices when she turned to face me – and she was holding a red-and-white-striped maraca. She was using it as a pretend microphone. My sister had brought along three differently coloured maracas to use on the dance floor.

My cousin and I locked eyes and then looked at the maraca. We were dumbstruck. The maraca was exactly the object Nell had described. And my cousin was dancing like nobody was watching, just as Nell had said. In my journal back at home I had unwittingly drawn an exact replica of the maraca my cousin was holding.

It was an amazing, inspiring and truly beautiful moment for us both. It gave us both such incredible joy and an unbelievable sense of connection to Nell.

During the car ride home, I told my husband and children about what had transpired. I often feel my skills as a medium are a little hard to comprehend, but I knew this occurrence not only validated Nell's message to my cousin but also validated my skills as a medium. It was a gift from Nell to me to help my family accept my gift and understand where this gift would lead me.

There was an illustration of the maraca in the journal I kept in my bedside drawer, which I'd drawn before leaving. As soon as we arrived home, I showed my family the drawing. We all agreed it was extraordinary. It gave us great comfort knowing that Nell and all our loved ones in spirit are still present; still guiding us from above.

This night, this occurrence also really helped me. It gave me such unwavering proof that spirit was communicating with me. It helped me to trust in that and trust in myself. I didn't need to second guess myself and my gift any more. I didn't have to hide that part of myself. I had a gift which could bring such peace and comfort to others. Who was I to stand in the way of that? I was passing on the gift of love; from one yolk to another. All I needed to do was trust in that and trust in the process. I was trying to help, to inspire and to heal. I had and still have an overwhelming sense of gratitude for this gift.

I will never forget that night and the wonderful, uplifting joy I felt.

I believe we all have the ability to tap into this gift, and that we are receiving signs and signals all the time. We hear a song on the radio that reminds us of a loved one exactly at the moment they are in our thoughts. A flower blooms in the garden precisely on the date of a loved one's anniversary or birthday.

Many of us have this sense, these feelings that our loved ones are still keeping an eye on us, still watching over with love and support. These feelings bring us comfort and peace.

Leaving

Run to the moon and back
Tell all the stars you're leaving
Mop up the tears, open the blinds
No room left for grieving

Picture your eyes full of laughter
A smile on your beautiful face
Hear your whisper in the wind
I'm in a much happier place

Plant the seeds of your life
Adorn your space with flowers
The grass will continue to grow
As we miss you by the hours.

BERNADETTE SOMERS

The story of John

I believe all writers want permanence for their work and I believe this epitomises John, an author who wrote several books in his lifetime.

I did not know John while he was alive, but as a writer who shares the same desire for permanence, it is so fitting that I share his story.

The process of searching for a publisher for my book was incredibly easy. A series of recommendations and synchronicities led me to Michael, a publisher and writer who had followed his father John's love of writing and books.

As luck and fate would have it, I made contact with Michael through a friend's recommendation, and a fortuitous gap in his work schedule enabled me to begin collaborating with him immediately.

I had my first meeting with Michael, which was held in the front room of his home, a room he used as his office.

On entering the room I was immediately struck by the presence of his father, John. I felt John's presence in the office space, in the pictures on the wall, his books and his writing. I did, however, feel Michael had kept some of his dad's memory locked away in the past.

On his desk, Michael had selected some of his published books that might be of a similar ilk to the book I was looking to publish, the book you are now reading. Michael suggested I look at a religious book that might be of interest. I looked at Michael with a direct gaze and told him that my book was not about religion, it was about connection.

As we continued to chat, Michael made reference to his father John, and mentioned that he had been inducted into the Catholic seminary as a young boy but left the priesthood as a young man.

He showed me his photo, and a painting on his office wall depicting his father's study full of books. I immediately felt that Michael was beginning to connect more with his father's memory, bringing that memory from his past into the present.

Michael then left the room to get me a copy of his father's book. I instantly heard John in my thoughts, urging me to choose Michael to be my publisher so that Michael could learn to connect more with him in the present. I instinctively knew there was something playing out for both Michael and myself, and that I had to publish my book with Michael.

I felt so strongly that John was telling me that Michael's anti-religious views were now interfering with his son's ability to connect with him. John felt that Michael needed to go through a doorway in order to fully honour his memory. He felt his memory had been wrapped in religion and placed in the memory box of the past. Yet, paradoxically, John's presence in his son's life, his writing and his home was so profound.

I realised that Michael was going to learn to reconnect with his father's memory through publishing my book. I also realised it was so important to share the message that remembering a loved one who has passed has little to do with religion and everything to do with connection. If we think about, talk about and remember our loved ones in the present, their memory stays with us.

Writers want permanence for their work and their memory. It's fitting that John is remembered in the pages of this book and indeed all of his own books, and that the process of me writing and publishing my book enabled me to honour another author in John.

May that serve to give him permanence.

YOLK PRACTICES

So where to from here?

How can you implement what you have learnt?

How can you start on your own yolk journey?

Here is your starting point to put into action the code you have discovered in the book.

Here is how to put it all into practice.

15 minutes

First, you have to become acquainted with finding yourself some quiet time.

You have to turn down the noise and stop the rushing.

You have to *commit* to a daily practice of sitting in silence and doing nothing.

You have to go inwards if you are to move forward.

You have to tap in.

This is your starting point.

You must find as a *minimum* 15 minutes a day to sit in a quiet room; no distractions, no noise, no fuss.

Light a candle if you want, grab a cushion, get comfortable and cosy. But not too cosy, or you may drift off to sleep.

Your phone is not welcome, so leave it somewhere it won't disturb or distract you.

Focus on your breathing. Breathe in and slowly breathe out; focus, and notice if you eventually settle into the flow and rhythm.

Take your time. Don't expect miracles. Go gently and see where it leads you.

You will eventually and gradually allow yourself to just *be*.

No excuses: 15 minutes every day. This is your starting point.

Journal

Second, buy yourself a notebook or journal, write today's date and note it as your start point.

Then write the following headings, leaving lots of room underneath:

- TAP IN (LOVE YOUR YOLK)
- SHOW UP (EXPRESS YOUR YOLK)
- STRETCH (CULTIVATE YOUR YOLK)

These are the lists you have written following the practices from earlier in the book. They are the answers to the questions your *yolk* asked you. These are the areas that need to be addressed.

The whispers of your yolk.

You are now going to write them in this journal and you are going to re-read these lists every day in your 15 minutes.

You need to re-write your *action* lists and brainstorm how you can action the changes required to love, express and cultivate your yolk.

Without looking back and reviewing on a regular basis, you won't notice progress and you won't stay on track.

Ask for guidance, ask for help, begin to attract into your orbit what you need to make change.

Visualise all is achieved, all is in balance. Spend the last few minutes of your 15 minutes imagining and feeling like it is your reality.

Put out the positive vibes, the positive energy.

Start the positive thoughts that will change your mindset and work with you to create change.

Believe there is a better way and that you have already found it in this book. Now you are going to *action* it.

Believe you can do whatever it takes.

You have come this far. You have the code. It's now your chance to use it.

Believe me when I say this book is infused with the energy to manifest your transformation. My guidance system has led me to write this book for *you*.

It speaks just to *you* and for *you*.

I have been given the code to share with *you*.

It will work. It will transform you if you allow it.

What arises from the pages of this book is destined to awaken you.

Try this:

Ask for guidance. Ask what you need to learn today.

Then hold this book in your safe hands and allow it to open to any page in any chapter. See what you have been guided to read. See what the message is for you.

I do this often and I am amazed at what I am directed to read, amazed at what page the book shows me. I feel as if the book is talking directly to me, even though I wrote it.

So *please* do your lists, find your 15 minutes, and imagine me there with you, coaxing you through every step.

Imagine all your everlasting yolks, your departed loved ones championing you and sending you love and support.

Talk to them and ask for their help. I promise you they will.
I promise you they hear your every word. I promise you they are just waiting in the wings, waiting to be asked. Watch out for your own synchronicities and signs; try to feel their guidance by tuning into your intuition.

Use this faith to inspire and uplift you. Use it to propel you forward.

You will be amazed at what unfolds. You will get the help you need.

Please email me your stories of how this magic unfolds for you (bernadette@bernadettesomers.com), and please email me your own stories of how your departed loved ones send you signs so I can honour them in my next book. Or, post them on Instagram: #yolk___.

I cannot wait to witness your transformation and to hear your story.

Conclusion

FAST TRACK TO your funeral. You see a room full of family and friends. You feel a great sense of love in the room for you, the departed. Someone near and dear to you is delivering your eulogy. Tears are being shed, memories relived, and smiles are interspersed with tears. Love engulfs the space and all in it.

The words of the eulogy describe your yolk, which has been encouraged as a child. It describes how throughout your life you loved, expressed and cultivated your yolk. It describes the best parts of you, who you were, your essence, all your very best bits. Your kindness, your loving nature, your God-given talents and authentic qualities; the stories, the examples, the very core of who you were. Your eulogy describes how you lived your life following a very simple code.

A code that you followed which enabled you to live a happy life and forge meaningful connections with others. The code taught you to love and accept yourself, in all your authenticity and glory. You believed you were loveable and worthy of all life's blessings.

You loved your yolk.

The code taught you to never let fear prevent you from living your life to its fullest potential. You braved vulnerability and never stayed small. You utilised all your potential and seized every opportunity. You achieved everything you wanted to in your lifetime because you believed you could.

You expressed your yolk.

The code taught you to engage in creative pursuits and do all the practices that kept you feeling connected and balanced. It taught you to trust in the bigger picture at play during your life, which showed you life was happening *for* you and not *to* you.

You cultivated your yolk.

As your eulogy draws to its conclusion, every person in the room feels the presence of your everlasting yolk. They remember you with love and admiration. Your life's journey of connecting within has enhanced your connection with everyone.

Your memory shines so much brighter because of the way you lived your life, because of this code you followed.

How you are remembered is in alignment with how you lived your life, with your yolk leading the way. Now your everlasting yolk lives on, an eternal light shining your brightness.

This was your code. Love your yolk. Express it. Cultivate it. Let this be your eulogy. Let this be your reality. Let this be your journey home.

I hope in the pages of this book you have found clarity, and you have stopped and reflected. I hope that through learning how to tap in, show up and stretch, you have learnt the absolute importance of having a shell.

You cannot tap into what's within without getting past the shell. You cannot show up unless you step out from within the shell. You cannot stretch unless you have something to stretch out from – the shell.

A life experience needs the shell, the constraints, the limitations, the confines from which to expand; that is growth, that is evolution. The yolk and the shell make up you, all your parts, all your majesty.

CONCLUSION

Living in true alignment is when your yolk works through the limitations of your shell. True enlightenment is when you have made peace with your shell, when you see its necessity for your spiritual growth.

I hope this book has enabled you to look into the reflection of your own very existence and see it with new eyes; new eyes that view the world brightly and with a new, sharp sense of clarity. I hope with this clarity you see yourself and the world differently, that you now can see the rhyme and reason behind all things and all events.

I hope you sense that you are both the leader and are being gently led, and that the new road ahead of you is clearly signposted with trust. I hope you now realise this road has always been available and accessible to you.

I hope you are beginning to see you can untangle yourself from whatever holds you back, be it fear, judgement, guilt or shame. I hope you know you are the master of your own destiny and can achieve whatever it is you so desire if you have self-love and self-belief.

I hope you now see all roadblocks as opportunities, all obstacles as lessons, every day as progress, every hour as a blessing, every moment as vital, every second as precious. I hope you believe that what truly matters is what is happening right now, and I so hope you sense that in this very moment all is well.

I hope you believe that loving your yolk will bring you the joy and freedom you are searching for. I hope you have learnt that expressing your true yolk sets you free and empowers you to create whatever future you dream for yourself, using the shell as the constraint to rise above.

I hope you learn the practices of cultivating your yolk to bring you greater peace and balance in your life. I hope you understand a yolk well cultivated in this lifetime creates an everlasting yolk always remembered by those you leave behind.

My greatest hope is that all of us, all of humankind, live in this manner, love in this manner, act and behave in this manner. For it would serve us all equally.

Our connections to each other would strengthen. This basic blueprint of love and loving would set us free.

This is my hope for us.

This is my wish.

May all of your beautifully crafted, soft and golden yolks shine brightly in their unified majesty to light the planet like the stars.

Until they soar as spirits to another plane of light and love.

That awaits us ... all.

www.ingramcontent.com/pod-product-compliance
Lightning Source LLC
Chambersburg PA
CBHW071451080526
44587CB00014B/2069